T0157035

WEAPONS OF MASS DISRUPTION

THE TERRORIST EFFECT:
WEAPONS OF MASS DISRUPTION

THE DANGER OF NUCLEAR TERRORISM

JAMES WILLIAM JONES

AND

JOHN R. HAYGOOD

iUniverse, Inc.
Bloomington

THE TERRORIST EFFECT:
WEAPONS OF MASS DISRUPTION
THE DANGER OF NUCLEAR TERRORISM

iUniverse books may be ordered through booksellers or by contacting:

iUniverse
1663 Liberty Drive
Bloomington, IN 47403
www.iuniverse.com
1-800-Authors (1-800-288-4677)

Because of the dynamic nature of the Internet, any web addresses or links contained in this book may have changed since publication and may no longer be valid. The views expressed in this work are solely those of the author and do not necessarily reflect the views of the publisher, and the publisher hereby disclaims any responsibility for them.

Any people depicted in stock imagery provided by Thinkstock are models, and such images are being used for illustrative purposes only.
Certain stock imagery © Thinkstock.

ISBN: 978-1-4620-3932-6 (sc)
ISBN: 978-1-4620-3933-3 (ebk)

Printed in the United States of America

iUniverse rev. date: 08/09/2011

TABLE OF CONTENTS

Prologue

OTHER BOOKS BY JAMES WILLIAM JONES

Triple Crossed
(ISBN 978-1-4502-5852-4)

The Last Viking
Wilhelm's Thousand-Year Quest to Regain Valhalla
(ISBN 978-0-595-51095-5)

ACKNOWLEDGMENTS

This book could not have been written without the help of many people too numerous to mention by name. The licensees we interviewed provided valuable insight into the daily operations of sites that use radioactive materials. We appreciate the opportunity to meet with the FBI and other law enforcement and regulatory officials who are working diligently to prevent such terrorist events. Charles R. Meyer, who was a co-worker in the initial phase of our research, continues to be a tremendous resource contributing from his vast knowledge of physics and nuclear materials. Dr. Robert Nickell, one of the investigators in the Sloan Foundation Grant that supported our research, was, and continues to be, a contributor to the knowledge base that underlies this work. We especially appreciate the efforts of Reese Meisinger and the staff of ASME International. His organization provided a vehicle for the development of the methodology used to assess the risk posed by weapons of mass disruption and to evaluate risk management solutions.

This work would not have been possible without the financial support of the Alfred P. Sloan Foundation. Dr. Paula Olsiewski, Program Director, has contributed in numerous ways, including her moral support, her conviction that this work was important to this country, her contacts with the FBI and Interpol, and her technical suggestions. Paula's comments and suggestions are incorporated into our work and it is much better for that.

The patient and tireless work of my (Jones) long-suffering wife, Mary, is gratefully acknowledged. Her English degree was invaluable as she attempted to take the commingled (some might even say "comangled") prose of an engineer and a physicist and make it intelligible.

Finally, the authors assume all responsibility for any errors, omissions, or just plain shortcomings of this book. The wonderful folks mentioned above should not be blamed for our blunders. Their only mistake is to be associated with us in the first place.

James William (Bill) Jones John R. Haygood
Huntington Beach, CA Austin, Texas

The narrative scenarios used to illustrate how radioactive materials can be obtained and used are fictional. All of the characters, names, incidents, organizations, and dialogue in these fictional accounts are either the products of the authors' imagination or are used fictitiously. Any resemblance to persons living or dead is purely coincidental.

PROLOGUE

Ernie Hawkins turned right off Highline Avenue into Plainview Mall and drove across the deteriorating tarmac lot. *The message sign has lost another letter or two*, he thought. It read "PLAIN EW ALL". *It's pretty plain all right,* he mused.

The white parking lines were faded and Johnson grass, encouraged by spring rains, fought to reclaim the cracked asphalt surface. Ernie pulled his car under the shade tree that stood near the north entrance, stepped out of the car, and stretched.

No new tenants. Why doesn't this surprise me, he thought as he removed his radiation survey and sampling equipment from the trunk.

Attaching his scintillation detector, Ernie turned on the survey equipment and started walking slowly toward the buildings.

Nothing, he thought as he read the gage. *I haven't gotten a reading for years. Maybe I ought to buy this place. I bet I could get it for a song. Course, what would I do with it? Nobody wants to come here now. It's a damn shame.*

As Ernie took soil and surface samples, he began to think about the first time he covered this ground with his monitor. It was almost thirteen years ago, he remembered. It was about this time of the year. He had been driving back to the radiation control office in Arlington on his way from Park Place Hospital, when he heard a news flash on the radio: "A large explosion has occurred at Plainview Mall. It appears be in the food court area. There is no information, yet, on injuries. KDAL has a mobile unit on the way. We should have details momentarily. This is Jane

Darling reporting live from Chopper 1." He could remember the announcement word for word. It had changed his life.

Ernie unlocked the chain on the building entrance and propped both doors open. *Not much light in here*, he thought. As he walked down the wide corridors of the deserted mall taking readings, he pondered the futility of his mission. He hadn't found significant radiation here for years and years. *I don't know why I have to keep doing this. Everything was cleaned up six months after the incident. At least I only have to do it every quarter now.*

He would never forget receiving the call from Austin on his cell phone.

"Ernie, get your equipment and get over to Plainview Mall. There was a large explosion and first responders have detected radiation. We need someone over there to check it out!"

The memory of that night came flooding back. He had just pulled into the office parking lot. It was about closing time and most people had already left for the day. Becky, the radiation control assistant, was still at her desk. Ernie remembered saying, "Becky, call all of the inspectors and tell them we may have a problem at Plainview Mall. There was an explosion and the fire department reports radiation there. Tell 'em we may all have to respond, so be ready." He grabbed his emergency response case and left. *Fifteen miles through rush hour traffic*, he remembered. *I thought I would never get here. That was one long night*, he recollected.

The initial explosion in the food court had killed twelve people and injured 27 others. The radiation levels were not lethal and he had gotten about half a year's worth of his allowable annual dose that night. Some of the police and firemen were afraid to go into the area so Ernie had helped carry out the injured. Almost 200 emergency personnel were contaminated.

It was the worst radiation incident up to then, he recalled. *Now, it seems small. We had about 600 civilians contaminated,* he remembered as he walked past the silent escalator. *It's funny. No one has even vandalized the place. I guess even punks are afraid of radiation. The ironic thing is there isn't any radiation.*

Ernie finished his routine check and headed back to his car. *What a shame. The whole area is like a ghost town. I'm sure glad I don't own property around here.*

CHAPTER 1

THERE WILL BE AN ATTACK

This book was written to fill what the authors perceive as a gap in public awareness regarding the possibility of a terrorist event involving radioactive materials. We believe such an event is not just a possibility but, given time, is a virtual certainty.

There are more than 21,000 locations in the United States that use or store enough radioactive material to terrorize us and change our lifestyle. This material cannot be used to make an "atomic bomb" but an improvised explosive device that disperses this radioactive material can strike terror into anyone who does not understand the actual danger of such an event. Radioactive materials may be the ultimate terrorist weapon; knowledge and awareness can blunt this serious threat.

The earthquake, followed immediately by a tsunami in Japan (the Japan event), graphically illustrates how the public, and certainly the media, perceives danger due to radioactive materials. While there were over thirty thousand casualties caused by "natural" events, the specter of danger to radioactive materials released by the nuclear plants was by far the biggest media story. This fear reverberated around the world and Germany immediately responded by revoking nuclear plant life extensions for seven of its seventeen reactors. Political elections in Germany were affected by the news. The United States is "reevaluating" the design of existing plants and reviewing the design basis for the next generation of nuclear power reactors. In fact, many countries promptly announced their intention to reevaluate their nuclear plants and operating procedures.

In the final analysis, how many lives were lost to radiation in Japan? The answer is none. How many lives were shortened by radiation exposure? Officials, technicians, and critics will disagree on the exact number, but everyone will agree it will be significantly less than in the Chernobyl incident where thirty-one deaths are directly attributed to the accident and the World Health Organization (WHO) estimates 4,000 deaths will be eventually be attributable to the Chernobyl incident.[1] As of 2008 only 64 deaths are known to have been directly caused by (non-war) radiation.[2] The authors are not aware of any additional deaths since that time.

These numbers pale in comparison to the 30,000 lives lost in Japan resulting from the natural disasters. The 2004 Indian Ocean earthquake and resulting tsunami claimed over 230,000 lives in fourteen countries. The deaths and suffering caused by these natural disasters, not to mention the cost of rebuilding, are orders of magnitude greater than for the Chernobyl event.

So, why are people much more afraid of incidents involving radioactive materials than of natural events? It is a well-established fact people are more afraid of some things than others. Experts in risk assessment have studied this phenomenon and a qualitative measure can be defined as "Risk Tolerance". We are typically more tolerant of risks "we can control" than risks out of our control.

---

[1] Chernobyl: The true scale of the accident 20 Years Later-A UN Report Provides Definitive Answers and Ways to Repair Lives Joint News Release WHO/IAEA/UNDP http://www.who.int/mediacenter/news/releases/2005/pr38/en/index.html

[2] United Nations Scientific Committee on the Effects of Atomic Radiation, http://en.wikipedia.org/UNSCEAR

It is a well-known fact approximately 40,000 people die every year in automobile accidents. Most of us believe it is safer to fly by commercial airline than to drive. Yet, there are many people who will not fly in an airplane but will drive thousands of miles on highways where the risk of dying is much higher. (Former Oakland Raider football coach and television personality John Madden is probably the most well-known example.)

Why? One reason seems to be people believe they can control their risk when driving but lose control when flying. Never mind if someone swerves into your lane and hits you head-on. You can't avoid the impact and you will probably become a statistic for next year's traffic report.

We fear some diseases more than others. We tolerate overweight but quit smoking. We fear snakes but keep pit bulldogs in our houses with our small children. These examples may be termed "irrational comparisons".

Possibly the greatest irrational comparison of all is the fear of radiation.

While watching the media coverage of the Japanese catastrophe, the authors were struck by the number of times reporters implied the information being released by government officials was not accurate and probably underestimated the "true" danger. No matter how forthcoming officials were, the media continued to warn the public that withholding information could be a way to prevent panic. Radiation levels were reported as being 5 or 10 times normal. The fact that normal radiation levels are incredibly low and the human body can tolerate levels much higher without suffering damage was seldom mentioned. In addition, there was no one in the so-called "high radiation" areas to be exposed. Attention by the news media quickly turned from the earthquake and tsunami, which caused thousands of deaths and injuries, to the troubled nuclear plants, which caused no deaths and few injuries. In short, the media loves to create an ongoing news event, which will arouse concern. Radiation from nuclear materials is a great choice for the media. Neither the media nor the general public understand the actual danger. "Experts" are trotted out to opine on the subject endlessly, often giving misleading, even erroneous, information. Opponents of nuclear energy are thrilled to point out the inherent dangers of radiation and thus promote their cause, i.e., eliminating the use of nuclear power and radioactive materials.

Following the Japanese earthquake /tsunami/nuclear emergency event, one well-known reporter of a major television news network asked a nuclear expert if Japan was well enough equipped to deal with the incident. The expert explained with earthquakes and tsunamis being fairly frequent phenomena visited on Japan, and with their experience in dealing with nuclear emergencies through drills and exercises, he concluded Japan was probably one of the most experienced and capable countries in the world in dealing with these emergencies.

The reporter then asked, "So, what went wrong?"

The expert responded by saying, "That's like asking what went wrong when a large asteroid crashes down on a major city."

This exemplifies the propensity for members of the news media to sensationalize events, often through their own ignorance. Governmental agencies and the nuclear industry are accused of downplaying the actual danger to mitigate damage to their interests, and cannot be trusted to tell the truth. What a great news story!

Now assume we have a terrorist event which involves the spread of radioactive materials. The public risk tolerance of any terrorist event is much lower than for the same consequences caused by an accident or natural event. The thinking seems to go like this: "I can understand a natural event and plan for it. Accidents happen and always will. However, good planning and hard work can reduce accidents and/or their consequences. A terrorist event is completely out of my control."

Now, combine this thinking with the inherent distrust of authorities and government. Add in the element that the public does not understand the actual danger of exposure to radioactive materials: how much radiation is too much, or how do you clean up contaminated sites? Throw in the erroneous idea that death from radiation is so much more horrific than death from anything else. This combination of uncertainty and the opportunity to create panic provides a dangerous formula for terrorists to develop weapons of mass disruption.

This book is intended to provide answers to some of these important questions. Questions such as:

- How could this happen?
- Where could they get material?
- How dangerous are the materials?
- What can I do to prevent an attack?
- What can I do to protect myself and my family if there is an attack?

However, before you read further, and learn the answers to these questions, it is important to establish something at the outset. The authors do not have an agenda. We have nothing to gain or lose by telling the unvarnished truth. We do not represent government (local, state, national), big business, insurance companies, utilities (especially nuclear utilities), consultants working for any of the preceding, university professors, most of whom have research sponsored by one of the preceding, lawyers who are trying to find a way to cash in, law enforcement, or the media.

You will find detailed scenarios of theft and misuse of radioactive materials. The authors, however, have deliberately omitted certain steps, aspects, and information so as to prevent any person from being able to use the information in this book to create an explosion with radioactive material, or to otherwise obtain and use radioactive material to harm anyone. The authors, too, live in the United States. There will be criticism of this book because we have explicit examples of how a terrorist can obtain and deploy radioactive materials.

Do not be naive. Our enemies are bright, well educated, and devoted to destroying our way of life. We must assume they know everything we know and more. The 9/11 attacks were not anticipated by our security agencies. If someone had published such a scenario before the attacks, it might have changed airline policy regarding highjackers. The prevailing wisdom before 9/11 was to let the highjackers have control of the plane and when they received ransom and/or asylum in another country, the passengers would be released. Now we know better. In this age of information, it is virtually impossible to prevent our enemies from knowing how to harm us.

The authors hope to better inform the public, believing a better informed public can better withstand the challenges of terrorist attacks. We can fight back with knowledge and an understanding of the true dangers. Overreacting to an attack will only further the cause of the terrorist. If we can reduce public overreaction by even a small percentage, this book will be a success.

In the following chapters, we will be presenting various attack scenarios that describe how terrorists could utilize radioactive materials found in medical, industrial, and academic (MIAN) operations to create weapons of mass disruption. The scenarios we have chosen are realistic, viable, and illustrate numerous ways a terrorist could use these materials to disrupt our lives, change the very way we live and work, and exact a heavy monetary consequence. We will attempt to dissect these scenarios and describe how they can be avoided. More importantly, we hope to show the actual, long term, danger is much lower than most of us realize. Most terrorist events involving radioactive materials can be avoided entirely or quickly remediated. We can return to our normal routines with little or no danger to our health. The thrust of terrorism is to strike fear into our hearts, but Franklin D. Roosevelt's saying, "We have nothing to fear but fear itself" applies here. Most important of all, we must learn to avoid panic.

We must react in a rational, informed manner. Unless we do, the terrorist will win.

CHAPTER 2 ▬▬▬▬▬▬▬▬▬▬▬▬▬▬

WHAT IS A WEAPON OF MASS DISRUPTION?

Blake Smith jumped as he heard footsteps coming down the deserted hallway. He sat straight up in his chair and shook his head as if to shake off the fatigue he was feeling. A glance at the large clock over his desk revealed it was only two-thirty. Four and a half hours left before his replacement arrived. It was going to be a long night. He recognized the young orderly approaching his desk.

"Hi, Mo. I haven't seen you all night."

"I've been up on the fifth floor. There was a mess to clean up as soon as I got to work tonight. Every time I just about finished one thing, somebody spilled something or there was you know what to carry. I am ready for my break. How is it going down here?"

"It's pretty quiet tonight. We had a couple of bad car wrecks come in about midnight and then it dropped off. They might be out of ER by now. Ramirez is over there. I suspect he'll be there most of the night. Same ol', same ol'."

"I don't know Ramirez. Is he new?" inquired Mo.

"He only works a few nights a month. He normally works downtown traffic on the morning shift. He likes to pick up an extra buck when he can. He has three kids and another on the way. It must be pretty hard to make ends meet on a city cop's pay. His wife don't work either."

"How about a cup of coffee, Blake? I'm going back and get me some. Cream and sugar?"

"Why not? I think I've drunk enough to float a battleship already, but it's hard to stay awake the first night on the job after a couple of days off. I can't ever sleep before I come to work and as soon as I get here I feel like I could sleep on a bed of nails."

"Tell me about it," responded Mo sympathetically. "This is my last night. I have tomorrow and Wednesday off. Hand me your cup. Be right back with some coffee."

Mo walked resolutely back to the kitchen area and made sure the swinging door closed behind him. He filled Blake's cup about three-quarters full and then added half-and-half out of the refrigerator. He tore off the tops of three packets of sweetener and dumped them into the cup.

That should kill the bitter taste of the pills, he thought.

Mo walked to the door and cracked it, checking the hallway. *No one around tonight*, he mused. *Maybe Blake will have a long nap.*

Mo pulled the plastic bottle out of his pocket and twisted off the childproof cap as he walked back to the counter. He carefully dropped three oval, white pills into Blake's coffee cup, replaced the cap, and stirred the mixture. *Three Xanax should relax old Blake. His next stop will be a visit to Morpheus.*

"Here you go, Blake. This should fix you up," said Mo as he handed the mug to Blake. "Cheers," he said as he raised his coffee in mock celebration.

Mo sat at the side of the desk and began to carry on a very boring conversation as he did most nights on his break. Mo had only worked at the hospital for six weeks and he already exhausted topics for conversation. Blake began to slump in his chair. He sipped more coffee and appeared surprised to notice it was almost gone.

"Why don't you lay your head down for a few minutes?" asked Mo. "I will let you know if anything happens. It should be quiet for a while on the fifth floor. All the patients are asleep and the nurses are doing paperwork."

"Wake me up in fifteen minutes. A catnap would help. I'm on my break anyway," slurred Blake as he laid his head on folded arms.

Blake was out like a light as soon as his head hit the desktop. Mo waited a few minutes to make sure and then stood and looked around the reception area. Blake's desk was off to the side of the entry and partially concealed from view by a partition to give him a little privacy. Mo reached carefully across and unhooked the ring of keys on Blake's belt. He stuffed the keys in his pocket as he glanced around again. There was no one in the reception area. There had never been an incident in the hospital, but the security program for radioactive materials required an armed guard.

So much for the rent-a-cop, thought Mo. *He isn't a bad old guy. I'm glad I didn't have to kill him.*

Mo walked briskly down the long hallway and opened the side door. There, across the parking lot, was the van, just as he knew it would be. He waived to the driver and stepped back inside to watch the hallway. When he heard the driver cut the engine, he looked both ways and opened the door again. The rear doors of the white Chevrolet service van were open and two swarthy men dressed in scrubs were unloading a gurney.

The men pushed the gurney into the hallway and started toward the elevator. This gurney was unusual in the fact that it was constructed of heavy pipe and painted white. Sitting on the gurney, covered with a white sheet, was a large backpack with enough explosives to destroy the entire wing of the hospital. Next to it was an M-16 he had recently purchased at a gun show. Mo had reworked the firing mechanism so it would empty the oversize magazine in less than a minute. The gurney was capable of carrying several thousand pounds. Mo had designed and built it himself and he was proud of it.

When the elevator door opened, Mo heaved a sigh of relief. No one on board. Now they would definitely get to the blood irradiator undetected. This was step one and it was almost completed. The ride up to the second floor seemed to take an eon.

Mo worried about Blake. *Would he stay asleep long enough? What if Ramirez decides to check on Blake? That's why I have the M-16*, he remembered.

The elevator doors finally opened on the second floor. *No lights. No one here. Good. So far so good.* Mo switched on his flashlight and sprinted ahead as his companions rolled the gurney across the polished floor. He stopped at the door to the irradiator facility and shined his light on the key ring. He knew the key. He had made the rounds with Blake several times. He had told Blake he wanted to get a job with security. The old man was helping him. *I'm glad I didn't have to kill him went through his mind again.*

The second door he came to was locked but he knew which key fit. What he didn't know was the security code to punch into the pad on the wall beside the door. The alarm would go off at the downtown office of Pinkerton as soon as he opened the door. *Oh well, so be it. It will be too late when they get here one way or the other.*

Mo turned on the lights as soon as he entered the room. Now, it was a race to get the cobalt-60 out of the irradiator before security arrived. He threw back the sheet on the gurney, set the backpack carefully on the floor, and grabbed the pry bar.

"You set up the hoist frame, Kaz, and we will get this thing out. Yusuf, help me get the shield loose."

The pry bar and a two-pound sledge made short work of the cowling and the tungsten shielded container was visible. Mo hooked the come-along to the container and Kaz started turning the crank, reeling in the stout cable onto the drum. It took a couple of tries and a chisel to cut the mounting bolts, but the unit was soon free and transferred to the gurney. Mo placed the bag of explosives back on the gurney and they headed for the elevator. He looked at his watch. It had only been ten minutes since he set off the alarm.

We just might make it, he thought.

When the elevator reached the first floor, Mo turned toward Kaz and Yusuf, "Get this thing into the van. I'll be right there. If the police are waiting, blow it. I will see you in paradise."

Mo raced down the hallway and into the reception area. As he neared the security area, he could see Blake still lying motionless across his desk. The landline was ringing incessantly. As he reached the desk, he grabbed the phone, and breathlessly spoke.

"Jay, here. Can I help you?"

"Where the hell have you been! I've been calling for ten minutes. Where's Blake?"

"He had to go to the bathroom. I work with him. I'll get him. Do you want to hold?"

"Is anything goin' on over there? We got a light on the board here and I need to know if I should notify the key holder?"

"Everything is OK here. There must be something wrong with the alarm. I'll have Blake call you when he gets back."

If I don't hear from him in two minutes, I'm callin'. Go get his sorry ass and tell him to call me."

"I'll tell him. Bye."

Mo hurried down the hallway and outside. Kaz and Yusef were in the van waiting with the rear doors closed and the motor running.

"OK, men. We got this far," said Mo as he climbed into the van. "Next stop, New York City."

The white service van pulled across the almost empty parking lot, paused at the light, and then turned up the ramp toward the turnpike. They shed their scrubs and headed toward the city.

* * *

An explosion rocked downtown New York City at exactly four-thirty a.m. First responders quickly discovered the area was highly radioactive. It would be many months before things could be back to what eventually might be called "normal".

* * *

The preceding scenario illustrates how radioactive materials, which normally provide life saving benefits, can be used by terrorists to cause correspondingly great damage. We will refer to these materials as Mass Disruption Weapons (MDW), not to be confused with weapons of mass destruction (WMD). The difference between the two will be obvious. Most of us are familiar with WMD from the lead-up to the Iraq war and the subsequent fruitless search for WMD after the United States invaded Iraq. WMD come in many forms, from biological weapons to chemical weapons to the most dreadful of all, nuclear weapons. Weapons of mass destruction are intended to destroy lives and infrastructure in catastrophic events. Such weapons are seldom employed because the threat of deployment is often enough to change the course of world events.

The use of WMD in the form of atomic bombs in Hiroshima and Nagasaki ended World War II. The threat of atomic weapons fueled the Cold War and the Cuban Missile crisis almost resulted in the deployment of atomic warheads in 1963. The threat of

WMD continues and there are numerous government programs in place to prevent such weapons from falling into the hands of terrorists and rogue nations. There is no doubt WMD continue to pose a great threat to the Unites States and our allies around the world. Numerous books and papers have been written on this subject. This book, however, is not about weapons of mass destruction.

The goal of the terrorist is actually very simple and exactly as the name implies. They strive to terrorize their enemies and cause lasting economic and psychological damage. A terrorist attack can fail to achieve its intended goal and yet cause great damage to their enemies. Hijacked United Airlines Flight 93, bound for Washington, D.C. on September 11, 2001, crashed in a field in southwest Pennsylvania near the small town of Shanksville. It did not reach Washington as planned, yet it was partially successful because it demonstrated the extent and complexity possible for an undetected terrorist mission. This reinforced the overall terrorist goals and revealed the vulnerability of then current airline security measures.

The heroic efforts of Flight 93 passengers undoubtedly saved countless lives by preventing the plane from reaching its intended target, however, subsequent changes to security and passenger screening are a lasting monument to the effectiveness of the Al Qaeda attacks. The cost of increased airport security is measured not only by the direct costs of employing the personnel of the Transportation Safety Administration, hiring and training air marshals, and purchasing screening equipment, and but also by the loss of productivity and individual freedom.

The September 11, 2001, attacks resulted in a quantum change in airline travel. It affected the type and quantity of substances we can bring on board the plane, restricted us from socializing with our friends and relatives as they embarked or disembarked at the gate, added at least one hour to travel times and subjected us to search and questioning which invades our privacy. We are now entered into databases, which contain our profiles. We cannot lock our checked baggage, making it more likely our possessions will be stolen.

Radioactive materials that can be used for disruptive purposes are available from many sources. More than 21,000 medical, industrial, and academic nuclear facilities in the U.S. are licensed to use radioactive materials, and there are many similar sites around the world. These materials are used for various purposes, including medical and veterinary treatments, industrial applications, and academic research. They cannot be used to make an atomic bomb and they cannot be transformed into weapons of mass *destruction*. However, in the hands of a terrorist they can be used as very effective weapons of mass *disruption*. A lapse in security could result in these highly radioactive materials falling into the hands of terrorists where they can be used for nefarious purposes. They could be used in a radioactive material dispersal device (RDD), a so-called "dirty bomb", or be released into the environment through other means. Under extreme conditions, they can cause fatalities, serious injuries, and environmental damage, which could require costly decontamination or abandonment of valuable locations. Deployment of an RDD could cause disruption of commerce, denial of critical services and infrastructure, or loss of access to public locations. A site where an RDD has been deployed will require time for assessment, decontamination, and reassessment until the radioactive material has been reduced to acceptable levels. The site would be rendered unusable during this process, which could take from weeks to years, depending on the radioactive material and the extent of dispersion.

As previously explained, an RDD is not a weapon of mass destruction, such as a nuclear warhead or atomic bomb that utilizes either fission or fusion of highly refined nuclear materials.

Rather, an RDD is a weapon which can result in mass disruption, a disruptive radiation device (DRD). While a DRD is unlikely to cause large numbers of fatalities or serious injuries, it could have devastating economic consequences caused by the denial of access to key critical infrastructure components.

The Times Square car bomb attempt on May 1, 2010, in New York, perpetrated by homegrown terrorist Faisal Shahzad, would have been hundreds of times more disruptive had he included radioactive materials in the improvised explosive device (IED). Even though the explosion did not occur, the mere presence of radioactive material has the potential to create panic. The negative public perception of radioactive materials makes them particularly attractive to terrorists. By definition, it is the goal of the terrorist to induce fear in an attempt to coerce governments for political or ideological gain. Fatalities or serious injuries are not necessarily the ends that terrorists seek.

The public fear of radioactive materials cannot be overstated. We do not have the capability to detect the presence of radioactive materials without appropriate sensors placed in critical locations. RDDs can spread radioactive materials in a highly populated area using improvised explosives. While the risk of fatalities is primarily due to the explosion itself, and the radioactive materials can be expunged from the area by well-known decontamination methods, the fear of residual effects will greatly limit commerce and result in costly security enhancements. If such events occur, it will be difficult to restore public confidence in government agencies tasked with preventing such events.

Radioactive material might also be used as a non-DRD weapon. Large radiation sources can be placed in locations to cause high exposures to members of the public as they go about their day-to-day business. For example, radioactive material used in industrial radiography to x-ray dense objects could be placed under a seat in a subway train in a large city. Persons sitting on the seat may be fatally exposed, while those sitting within a seat or two of the location could receive debilitating radiation doses. Further, radioactive material placed in soluble form could be introduced to food and/or water supplies. Some isotopes placed in food or water under the right conditions may cause fatalities and would surely cause serious illness.

In the terrorist attack scenario described at the beginning of this chapter, the most desirable goal of the terrorist team was achieved. A large quantity of a highly radioactive material (cobalt-60) was obtained by the terrorists, transported to the center of a major city (New York) and an RDD was successfully detonated. The terrorists may not have been apprehended and they may have escaped to strike again. The probability of achieving this "complete success" is probably low. However, the plan used by the terrorists contained numerous options or abort points that could have been utilized. For example, the attack would have been aborted if Mo did not neutralize the night shift guard or if the night duty police officer was in the same building. Presumably, Mo had worked at the hospital long enough to choose the best time and place for the attack. He also knew the routes of access and how to manipulate hospital staff that could have disrupted the attack. If the sleeping pills did not work, then Mo could have used force to eliminate the night watchman. If the mission was aborted in the event the night watchman did not fall asleep, nothing of their plan had been revealed and the mission could be attempted at a later time.

Once the gurney was inside the hospital, Mo had access to an automatic weapon. The probability of reaching the blood irradiator would have been very high and a suicide bombing would have scattered contaminating radioactive material. The ensuing fire would have further spread the cobalt-60 (Co-60) causing great damage and terror in the local area. It should be noted that fire would not reduce or consume the amount of radioactivity contained in the source, but it would greatly enhance its distribution. A fire would probably cause the radioactive material to be distributed more widely throughout the complex, but the resulting radiation levels would be somewhat lowered. The decontamination task would be greatly increased.

If the terrorist group had not been able to remove the shielded radioactive material container from the blood irradiator, and move the Co-60 to the truck, they could have exploded the device remotely and left the scene alive. Assuming they were successful in moving the Co-60 to the service van, they had both the bomb and the radioactive material inside the van. Any attempt to interdict them as they transported the material to New York City would have resulted in an explosion and spread of the radioactive material in the local area during an attempted apprehension by law enforcement officers. Many terrorists are willing to die for their cause, and it must be assumed they will detonate the IED rather than be thwarted.

Thus, it is obvious this scenario is difficult to prevent and there is a high probability of at least limited success. Even partial success would have costly ramifications. Detonation of the device in the hospital would not have caused as great a monetary loss as if it occurred in New York City, but even the temporary loss of the hospital facilities and the expense of decontamination and repair would be costly to the local economy. It would also cause significant psychological damage. This attack would result in greatly increased security costs at the target hospital and all similar facilities throughout the United States. The increased costs of security at thousands of locations across the country would probably be the most expensive of all consequences.

In a later chapter, we will explain why this event, while serious, should not cause panic or overreaction. The radioactive material that would be released by the explosion and possibly fire, poses little danger to the community. There should be no fatalities due to radiation and little or no long-term effects caused by the increase in background radiation while the site is being remediated. The residual radiation can be reduced to normal levels by well-known and proven techniques, which are routinely used by those who work with radioactive materials.

In short, the event would pose less of a threat than many naturally occurring events. However, we have to learn to control our impulse to panic and be terrorized by something we do not understand. This is the main purpose of this book, and if the authors are successful in their attempt to explain why you need not be afraid, everyone in the United States will be safer and less vulnerable to our enemies.

CHAPTER 3

UNDERSTANDING RADIOACTIVE MATERIALS

Before we discuss more ways terrorists can use radioactive materials to attack us, it is very important to understand how and where radioactive materials are used, why they are dangerous, and why some uses are more dangerous than others. We have all seen videos of the mushroom clouds formed when an atomic bomb explodes and we have witnessed, through photographs, the incredible destruction caused in Hiroshima and Nagasaki at the end of World War II. The inhabitants of these towns in Japan were subjected to massive blasts consisting of heat, pressure waves, and high doses of radiation. Many of the survivors received burns due to both the incredible temperatures generated by the explosion and the effects of radiation. In the case of an atomic bomb, the explosion is much more destructive than the radiation.

The materials found in medical, industrial, and academic sites, with which we are concerned herein, cannot be used to make an atomic bomb. There is just not enough of the right type of radioactive material and it is not sufficiently concentrated. More on this later, but be assured no one will be able to make an atomic bomb from MIAN materials.

Probably the second most familiar use of radioactive materials is for generating electricity in nuclear power plants. The United States alone has 104 operating nuclear plants and hundreds more are located in Europe, Asia, Russia, and other developed countries in the world. The recent events in Japan in which nuclear plants have been damaged by the extreme earthquake followed by a huge tsunami have reminded us of the dangers of radioactive materials used in these applications. In the following pages we will explain why MIAN materials are not nearly as dangerous as nuclear fuel as it is utilized in power plants.

The following discussion will explain what constitutes "radioactive" material and how it is used in these and other applications. Before reading the next section, the reader is encouraged to consult Appendix 1 for a more in-depth discussion on radiation and radioactivity. If you have a strong technical background in physics, the following will serve to provide a quick review and allow us to define terms we will use later.

There is a considerable difference between the radioactive material used in nuclear weapons and power plants and the radioactive material used in society's normal course of business. In order to cause radioactive material to react in a manner that emits a great amount of energy, as is done with nuclear power reactors and nuclear weapons, atoms that can readily *fission* are required. Fission is the process of an atom splitting and releasing energy. Only a very few radioactive materials can be used for this process. Some of these are capable of spontaneously fissioning (fissile materials), while others require being forced to fission by manipulation (fissionable materials). Fissile materials include uranium-233, uranium-235, uranium-238, plutonium-239, plutonium-240, plutonium-241, and thorium-232.

Some of the radioactive materials capable of fissioning have been used in routine or research processes, but their use was either limited or the quantities used were very small. Most isotopes in use today are not capable of fissioning. If they are not capable of fissioning, then they cannot be used to create a nuclear explosion.

When a fissile atom fissions, or is split, it releases photons and one or more neutrons. The atom itself transforms into two or more different atoms (fission fragments). If arranged properly, the released neutrons can interact with other fissile atoms and cause them to split. This process continues as a "chain reaction" until all of the atoms have transformed. When used in a nuclear power plant, whereby the chain reaction is controlled, the point of sustained chain reaction is "criticality". Techniques are used to control the numbers and energies of neutrons present to control the fissioning process. To allow it to proceed too rapidly would rapidly burn up the nuclear fuel and produce too much heat to control.

When used in nuclear weapons, the object is to cause rapid chain reactions and achieve maximum energy release. This is done by accumulating a "critical mass" (the smallest amount of fissile material needed for a sustained nuclear chain reaction) of the fissile material, and forcing it into a geometrical configuration for a minimum amount of time (microseconds) to cause and sustain a "super criticality". This is a very tricky process. High explosives are used to achieve the correct geometry and holding time. Even if the correct geometry were to occur accidently, as perhaps in a damaged nuclear power plant, the extreme heat would cause the material to expand and immediately lose the necessary geometry. The required holding time could not be achieved. This is why a nuclear power plant cannot explode in the same manner as a nuclear weapon.

The fissile material used in nuclear weapons is not a very large quantity, so one might wonder why a nuclear explosion produces so much radioactivity. The excess radioactivity is caused by a process called *neutron activation*. This is a process which induces radioactivity in materials caused by exposure to neutron radiation. It happens when atomic nuclei capture free neutrons and become heavier while entering excited states.[3] The resulting atoms are then radioactive. The source of these atoms is the material at the site of the explosion (ground, buildings, air, etc.). Since there are many atoms available, the result is a great deal of induced radioactivity following a nuclear blast.

A nuclear explosion generated by using fissile materials is an "atomic bomb". However, there is also a device called a "hydrogen bomb" (thermonuclear). A hydrogen bomb explosion is caused by fusing hydrogen atoms. It takes a great deal of heat and pressure for a minimum amount of time to fuse hydrogen atoms. To do this, an atomic bomb is used as the "igniter" for a hydrogen bomb. Thus for nuclear explosions, the very difficult task of creating a fission explosion is required.

Long before 9/11, there was great concern for the security of "bomb grade" or special nuclear materials. As early as 1981, one text advised: "One of the serious concerns about the rapidly expanding nuclear industry is the possibility of theft or diversion of what are called special nuclear materials (SNM)—Pu-239, fully enriched U-235, and U-233—for purposes of nuclear blackmail, illicit bomb manufacture, or other forms of terrorism. Much attention has been devoted to providing adequate safeguards against this eventuality, but continued and increased vigilance is undoubtedly called for. Stringent physical security measures (including locks, fences, alarm systems, etc.) are mandatory wherever SNMs are present. In addition, however, it is most important to have reliable accountability and control procedures for keeping track of the flow of SNM throughout the fuel cycle, with provisions for establishing material balance at each step."[4] All

---

[3]   Wikipedia, "Neutron Activation, downloaded 05/11/2011
[4]   G. Friedlander, J. Kennedy, E. Macias, and J. Miller, *Nuclear and Radiochemistry*, 3rd ed, p. 542, John Wiley & Sons, New York, 1981.

of these safeguards have been incorporated and, after 9/11, have been "beefed up" even more. The use of bomb grade materials by terrorists is highly unlikely.

In summary, none of the MIAN radioactive materials in use today are capable of causing a nuclear explosion. The few materials (fissile) that could be used are not readily available and the process of creating such an explosion with them is exceedingly difficult. For example, the media reports Iran has thousands of centrifuges running in secret locations. This is because they are apparently attempting to separate the fissionable isotopes of uranium from the "stable" isotopes. The action of the centrifuge causes the slightly heavier fissionable atoms to separate from the slightly lighter isotopes. Because the density (or weight) of these atoms is almost identical, this process takes many months and literately thousands of centrifuges to produce enough fissionable material to make one atomic bomb. This is an example of how difficult it is to produce "bomb grade" material. Further, nuclear power plants cannot accidently create a nuclear explosion, should they become damaged, because the radioactive materials contained in the fuel are not capable of sustaining a nuclear explosion.

There have been several events at nuclear power plants which have caused significant consequences. These include the Three Mile Island Nuclear Plant (1979), the Chernobyl Nuclear Plant (1986), and the recent Fukushima Nuclear Plant in Japan (2011). Why is an event involving a nuclear plant more severe than we can expect from a terrorist event? The answer to this question involves how nuclear plants operate. The following discussion of how nuclear reactors operate is based on what is called a *pressurized water reactor* (PWR), a drawing of which is shown.). The majority of all power plants in the world are PWRs.

However, the Chernobyl reactor, designed by the Russians, is a graphite core reactor and not a PWR. Graphite blocks contain the fissionable material and they are water-cooled. The Fukushima reactor operated by Tokyo Electric Power is a *boiling water reactor* (BWR). Boling water reactors also use water as a moderator and coolant. Three Mile Island is a PWR.

In what follows, an explanation will be presented for why the radioactive material in power reactors is more dangerous than for radioactive materials found in MIAN uses. While the details are different for each reactor type, the basic concepts involved are valid for all designs.

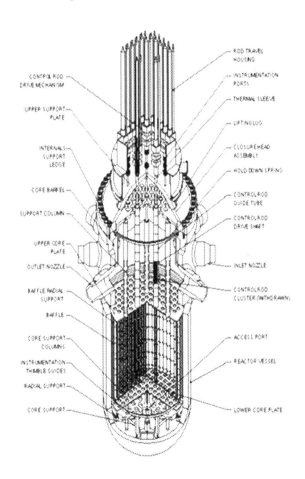

Nuclear power plants generate heat in the core. This heat is caused by nuclear materials breaking up because neutrons from one atom, which is "fissioned", strike other atoms, and cause these "target" atoms to break up. When this process continues unabated, it is known as a chain reaction. The fuel for a PWR reactor is a form of uranium, known as fissionable uranium, and consists of small pellets contained in long tubes. These tubes are made of a metal called *zircalloy*. This metal and is used because it does not inhibit the neutrons as they pass through the cylinder walls between *fuel rods*, as they are termed. The fuel rods are packaged in a square grid, and held in place by metal separators. The assembly of fuel rods, called a *fuel element,* is about one foot square and 12 feet long. Each fuel element contains from 200 to 300 fuel rods. The fuel element is the basic building block for the *core*, which consists of as many as 150 to 250 fuel elements. Thus, we have literally thousands (as many as 750,000) long cylinders containing uranium that are held in square arrays by the fuel elements. The fuel elements, placed inside the *reactor vessel*, make up the *reactor core*. The reactor vessel is a large, thick-walled (approximately 12 inches thick) steel container. The radioactive material in the fuel is an isotope of uranium and is constantly *decaying*, i.e., sending out neutrons as the material changes from one form to the next as described in Appendix 1. The core does not initially generate heat, however, because the neutrons are not plentiful enough to sustain a chain reaction. You need to add water!

When water is added to the reactor vessel, it "moderates" the neutrons, i.e., slows them down, giving them a better chance of hitting another atom. (The neutrons impact the lighter hydrogen atoms in water and are slowed down, or moderated. The slower neutrons have a higher probability of hitting another fissionable uranium atom.) Thus, water is key to sustaining the reaction. When the reactor is operating normally, the uranium atoms fission, i.e., break up into smaller components. This breakup produces heat. The newly released neutrons hit other atoms and they, in turn, break them up, producing more neutrons, and the chain reaction is sustained.

The water, which serves as the moderator, is also used to transfer the heat generated by the atomic reactions. Pumps circulate the water through heat exchangers; in this way, heat is removed from the nuclear reactor core. This is very similar to the way the radiator in your automobile works. The water pump circulates coolant through the engine block, which has been heated by the internal combustion of the gasoline. The radiator cools the water using air drawn in by the fan and the water recirculates back through the engine block to pick up more heat.

While this may seem complicated, it is very similar to most *conventional* power plants. In a coal-fired, natural gas, or oil-fired plant, the furnace burns the fossil fuel and heats water in tubes, which circulate water through the furnace. The heated water turns to steam and the steam drives a turbine wheel, which drives a electric generator, and we get electricity. The nuclear plant is the same except we are using the nuclear reactor core to generate heat to convert the water to stream rather than burning coal, oil or natural gas.

The difference, however, is that when you stop putting fuel in a conventional power plant, the heat stops. Turn off the gas and the plant shuts down. However, to shut down a nuclear plant, you must stop the chain reaction. We provide something called control rods in the core that will normally shut down the reaction. These rods are made of a special material that absorbs the neutrons and prevents the chain reaction from continuing.

However, the core still has a lot of heat left. It is somewhat like shutting off the burner on a stove. If you are using natural gas, the fire goes out immediately and your teakettle stops boiling. If you shut off an electric stove element, it takes more time for the heating to stop because the electric coil is still hot (the heating coils operate at temperatures over 1,000 degrees. The "red-hot" coil appearance can be used to determine the operating temperature.). As the heating coil cools down, the water will eventually stop boiling, but the residual heat in the coil continues to heat and boil water until it cools down below 212 degrees, the boiling temperature of water.

Nuclear cores are even harder to stop generating heat. After they have been operating for a long period of time they become highly radioactive. The fission process continues within the fuel elements after the chain reaction has been stopped. This residual activity generates a tremendous amount of heat. You must continue to cool the core and remove this residual heat. This is why the Fukushima reactor exploded. Cooling water could not be continually pumped into the reactor core because the electric pumps shut down due to loss of electrical power. The extreme heat in the core dissolves the water molecules, through *thermal decomposition*, into oxygen and explosive hydrogen gas. The gas continues to build up within the reactor until it is ignited and an explosion occurs.

Nuclear fuel does not last forever. The fissionable uranium will eventually "burn out" and the fuel element must be replaced. These retired elements, known as "spent fuel", are still highly radioactive, and must continue to be cooled or they will overheat. When the spent fuel elements are removed from the core, they are taken to the *spent fuel storage pool*, a large and deep concrete pool filled with water. There are typically hundreds of such "*spent*" fuel elements in the pool and the water in the pool must be continuously circulated to remove the residual heat emitted by spent fuel elements.

The recent Japan event resulted in loss of electric power to the nuclear plant. This triggered an automatic shut down and the control rods were driven into the core, stopping the chain reaction. However, the flow of cooling water through the core stopped because the main coolant pumps, which operate on electrical power, stopped pumping. Initially, the pumps operated on battery power. But after a time, they were to switch to large, emergency electric generators. Unfortunately, the tsunami had taken out the emergency generators. Because of the residual radioactivity, the core was still generating heat. This residual heat caused all of the water to boil out of the core. The core residual heat, if not removed, can cause the fuel elements to melt, including the zirconium alloy tubes. The melting of the tubes and the uranium pellets can produce hydrogen gas.

While the core was getting hotter, the spent fuel in the storage pool was also heating up since there was no cooling water being circulated. A further serious problem arose because water in the spent fuel storage area drained out through cracks in the concrete pool opened up by the earthquake. As the spent fuel was uncovered, it began to heat up and melt. The hydrogen was ignited, resulting in a hydrogen explosion. Radioactivity was released to the environment as well as inside the buildings that comprise the nuclear facility.

When the core of a nuclear reactor begins to melt, the radioactive material is no longer held in a nice array with spacing between the pellets and room for cooling water to circulate; the fuel can melt into a dense mass. When the fuel melts, it can reach a condition called the "critical" state. The fissionable uranium atoms are so close together they interact, allowing the chain reaction to be sustained. Now the core is generating great quantities of heat again and it can actually melt through the reactor vessel. This condition is known as a *core meltdown*, often referred to as the China Syndrome[5], a reference to the ridiculous assumption that the core could continue to melt a hole through the Earth and come out on the other side, in China.

There is a huge difference between a nuclear plant loss of coolant event and possible meltdown and the dispersal of radioactive materials such as are available in medical, industrial, and academic locations. The types of material a terrorist can obtain cannot produce self-sustaining reactions. They do not generate significant heat and thus cannot cause the type of event witnessed at Chernobyl or in Japan. The worst thing that can happen with MIAN materials is that they contaminate an area and must be cleaned up and the waste disposed of properly. Further, the quantity of radioactive material in a nuclear reactor is many, many times greater.

In summary, MIAN materials cannot explode as an atomic bomb. It is impossible. They do not generate heat like a power reactor. They cannot sustain a chain reaction. They are available only in relatively small quantities. They will not result in permanent contamination to metropolitan areas. They do not pose life-threatening levels of radiation unless they are ingested or in very close proximity to people.

MIAN materials are not weapons of mass destruction.

We can prevent them from becoming weapons of mass disruption.

---

[5]   This term was popularized by that great physicist and mathematician, and all-around intellectual, Jane Fonda, who "starred" in the movie of the same name. Fonda is also well remembered for her shrewd negotiations with the North Vietnamese.

CHAPTER 4 ▬▬▬▬▬▬▬▬▬▬▬▬▬▬▬▬

FEAR OF RADIOACTIVE MATERIALS

Using radioactive materials to incite terror and disrupt society is not a new idea. Terrorists have been interested in acquiring radioactive and nuclear material for use in malicious acts for many years.[6] For example, in 1995, Chechen extremists threatened to bundle radioactive material with explosives to use against Russia in order to force the Russian military to withdraw from Chechnya. While no explosives were used, officials later retrieved a package of cesium-137 the rebels had buried in a Moscow, Russia park.

Since September 11, 2001, terrorist arrests and prosecutions overseas have revealed that individuals associated with Al Qaeda planned to acquire materials for a RDD.[7] In 2004, British authorities arrested a British national, Dhiren Barot, and several associates on various charges, including conspiring to commit public nuisance by the use of radioactive materials.[8] In 2006,

---

[6] U.S. NUCLEAR REGULATORY COMMISSION, Backgrounder: Dirty Bombs (2007)
http://www.nrc.gov/reading-rm/doc-collections/fact-sheets/dirty-bombs.html

[7] U.S. NUCLEAR REGULATORY COMMISSION, Backgrounder: Dirty Bombs (2005).
http://www.nrc.gov/reading-rm/doc-collections/fact-sheets/dirty-bombs-bg.html

[8] Ibid

Barot was found guilty and sentenced to life in prison. British authorities disclosed Barot developed a document known as the "Final Presentation". The document outlined his research on the production of "dirty bombs", which he characterized as designed to "cause injury, fear, terror, and chaos", rather than to kill.[9] U.S. Federal prosecutors indicted Barot and two associates for conspiracy to use weapons of mass destruction against persons within the U.S., in conjunction with the alleged surveillance of several landmarks and office complexes in Washington, D.C., New York City, and Newark, NJ.

In a separate British police operation in 2004, authorities arrested British national, Salahuddin Amin, and six others on terrorism-related charges. Amin was accused of making inquiries about buying a "radioisotope bomb" from the Russian mafia in Belgium; and the group was alleged to have linkages to Al Qaeda.[10] Nothing appeared to have come from his inquiries, according to British prosecutors. While neither Barot nor Amin had the opportunity to carry their plans forward to an operational stage, these arrests demonstrate the continued interest of terrorists in acquiring and using radioactive material for malicious purposes.

Why radioactive materials?

The fear of the American public toward radioactive materials of all kinds is well documented. The Three Mile Island accident in 1979, the news of which touched off the evacuation of hundreds of thousands of residents, brought the building of nuclear facilities in the United States to a standstill in spite of the fact that no one inside or outside the plant was injured or killed. Of over one

---

[9]   Ibid
[10]   Ibid

hundred nuclear plants operating in the United States, not one has had a major or significant incident in three decades. While the only nuclear power plant deaths occurred at Chernobyl (31 deaths), a report by the nonprofit Clean Air Task Force states "over 13,000 deaths each year are attributable to fine particle pollution from U.S. power (coal) plants."[11] Most of the energy consumed in several other industrial countries, such as France and Japan, is generated mainly by nuclear energy. (The disposal of radioactive waste, a threat that is slow-moving and determined only over long periods of time, is fraught with similar anxiety, but this is a topic for another time.)

The cause of the nuclear standstill in the United States, grassroots theorists argue, is the fear on the part of the American public of the dangers of nuclear energy, and more precisely, the fear of radioactive materials. The recent Japanese event threatens to undo the slow progress toward resumption of construction of nuclear plants.

The public fear of radioactive materials is demonstratively an unfounded, or at least irrational, fear. The number of fatalities and injuries caused by radiation is diminishingly small compared to other risks we encounter every day. The risk of becoming a fatality in an automobile accident is orders of magnitude greater than the risk posed by exposure to radiation. While the public knows this intellectually, it does not prevent near panic reaction when there is a leak, however small, at a nuclear facility.

Before proceeding further, it is useful to establish how much radiation we can tolerate without causing any damage to the human body. The following statistics were taken from the May 2011 issue of Scientific American Magazine (sources listed as

---

[11] Clean Air Task Force, "Death and Disease from Power Plants", 05/11/2011. http://www.catf.us

National Council on Radiation protection and measurements, radiologyinfo.org). The average American is exposed to 3.1 millisieverts of radiation every year. This comes from so-called natural background radiation, and this we cannot avoid. It comes from cosmic rays from the universe, radon gas, and a multitude of materials we handle or ingest each year. This does not include medical procedures, such as will be discussed below, since it is judged that medical uses bring health benefits that outweigh the additional exposure.

Some sources of additional exposure (reported in millisieverts (mSv)) above background level include:

Airport Scanner (backscatter method)	.0001
Natural gas cooking (per year)	.0004
Arm x-ray	.001
Bone density x-ray	.001
Highway travel (per year)	.004
Dental x-ray	.005
Domestic airline flight (five hours)	.017
Smoking cigarettes (one pack/day for year)	.36
Mammogram	.4
Brain CT scan	2.0
Thyroid scan (nuclear medicine)	4.8
Brain scan (nuclear medicine)	6.9
Pelvis CT scan	10.00
Coronary CT angiography	16.00
Astronaut on space station (per year)	72.00
Fukushima emergency workers (per hour)	1.0
Airline pilot and crew (per year)	3.1
Nuclear power plant worker (per year)	1.9

Note: 1 mSv = 100 mrem.

Radiation experts recommend limiting public exposure to only 1.0 millisievert a year beyond background level. Japan recently reported they had increased the limit for emergency workers to 250 mSv a year. An emergency worker would "burn out" in approximately 250 hours of exposure or about six weeks working eight hour days, five days per week when in close proximity to the contaminated structures.

This table is actually very encouraging when you think about it. If we are exposed to a site where an RDD was exploded, assuming it is no worse than the Fukushima site, we would receive less than 1.0 millisievert of radiation exposure in an hour. Evacuation of the site would presumably take much less than an hour, thus the total amount of additional radiation would be much les than having a CT scan of the brain, pelvis, or heart. The exposure is approximately one-one hundredth (1/100) of the amount space station astronauts receive if they are in orbit for a year. To put this into perspective, the average exposure in the United States has risen from 3.6 mSv in 1980 to 6.0 in 2006.

As can be concluded from this comparison, the human body is constantly bombarded by radiation. We have evolved in an environment in which we are exposed to subatomic particles every second of our lives and we can tolerate moderate levels of radiation. When we have diagnostic CT scans, we willingly submit to radiation because it is the lesser of two evils; we believe finding diseases before they incapacitate or kill us is worth the risk of increasing our radiation dosage.

This is the same tradeoff we will have to make in the event of a terrorist attack that uses radioactive materials. Our first responders will evacuate us from the affected areas. They will cordon off zones of elevated radiation levels. A team of experts will decide how to best remediate the site. They will clean up the radioactive materials and properly dispose of them, as well as clothing and chemicals containing radiation. We will be allowed to return to the site when it is safe. It is our job to trust these experts and go back to business as usual. So, why are we afraid of radioactive materials?

There is a huge, almost unique, discrepancy between what experts say and how the public feels, a factor we will term "dread". It turns out that experts and the public calculate risk of harm in a drastically different fashion. Experts make use of what may be described as "absolute rationality"; the public uses "social rationality".[12]

The experts' statistical likelihood is calculated in a straightforward, rationalistic way: what is the statistical likelihood certain harmful outcomes will occur, and how harmful are those outcomes? For instance, what are the odds of dying while traveling by car from New York to Chicago? By plane? Although the statistical chance of dying in an automobile accident are considerably greater than the odds of experiencing death in an airline accident, far more fear the latter than the former.

The expert regards the public's fear as misguided and irrational. After all, if more deaths are produced by driving, on a mile-for-mile, passenger—for-passenger basis, then fear of flying, a safer mode of transportation, simply makes no sense. Hence, since such fear is anomalous and aberrant, the expert seeks out an explanation for it. There must be factors other than, and in addition to, statistical likelihoods of harmful outcomes, which make us more fearful of some threats than others.

The public fears threats to the extent they are perceived as involuntary, uncontrollable, unknown, unfamiliar, catastrophic, certain to be fatal, and delayed in their manifestation. Flying accidents (on commercial airlines) in contrast to driving or riding

---

[12]   Erich Goode and Nachman Ben-Yehuda, MORAL PANICS: The Social Construction of Deviance, Blackwell Publishing Ltd. (1e, 1994).

in a car are seen as involuntary and uncontrollable. The pilot and the weather determine outcomes, not the passenger.

Unknown and less familiar, catastrophic events are much more likely to be fatal when they do occur. Only in terms of latent, long-term, or delayed manifestations of harm are these two modes of transportation similar. It is not solely the odds of dying in an accident that generates fear of flying; it is the nature and mode of death that determines this dread. (However, if one has witnessed the mayhem wrought by a severe automobile accident first hand, dying instantly in a plane crash might indeed be the lesser of evils. Clearly, contemplating one's mode of death, especially when considering various accidental modes, is not a pleasant way to spend an evening and is not likely to add to one's reputation as a raconteur.)

Radiation exposure represents the extreme end of these perceptions of fear. Its risks are seen as involuntary, delayed, unknown, uncontrollable, unfamiliar, catastrophic, dreaded and potentially fatal. These underlying, and highly subjective characteristics that cause public fear of radiation are not included at all in expert's equations of risk. Radiation and other technological toxins "contaminate rather than merely damage; they pollute, befoul and taint rather than just create wreckage; they penetrate human tissue indirectly rather than wound the surface by assaults of a more straightforward kind."[13]

Incidents involving radiation "elicit an uncanny fear in us." People find radiation and other toxic substances significantly more threatening than most natural hazards and nontoxic technological hazards; they dread toxic substances far more intensely. Instead of assessing danger by calculating odds the way experts do, rationally as we should, the public regards radioactivity and other toxic

---

[13]   Ibid

substances as "naturally loathsome, inherently insidious—horrors that draw on something deeper in the human mind."[14] Toxic emergencies "really are different" from more routine accidents such as car crashes; "their capacity to induce a lasting sense of dread is a unique—and legitimate—property."

Probably the best way to account for this irrational bias is to consider a metric known as *risk tolerance*. Risk tolerance weighting provides a method of comparing absolute risk but includes factors that account for psychological considerations. It is well known that some types of risk are more easily accepted than others. Further, there are great differences between individuals with respect to the amount of acceptable risk. Thus, risk tolerance can be a measure of the individual differences in willingness to accept risk or a consensus of public willingness to accept various types of risk and risk levels.

The term "risk tolerance" is most commonly used in financial planning and describes a client's willingness to invest in risky opportunities as compared to safer, more predictable investments. One client might consider investing only FDIC insured savings accounts while another will buy stock in wildcat oil ventures or margin purchases in the commodity markets. There are free rock climbers, base jumpers, cliff divers, and the occasional Russian roulette participant. These are risk takers and they have a high tolerance for risk. Most of us are somewhere between phobia dysfunction and Evel Knievel.

Risk tolerance can also be applied in a broader sense to predict how the public will react to an event. Hurricane Katrina caused catastrophic damage to the Gulf Coast yet the vast majority of the original inhabitants remained in the affected area and began rebuilding their homes and businesses. Even though most

---

[14]   Ibid

recognize the fact that there is a high probability another large storm will hit the same area within their lifetime, most residents decided to stay and rebuild. Tornados are common in many parts of the Southern and Midwestern states, yet few people relocate when these events occur. Californians accept as fact that the "big one" (earthquake) is only a matter of time.

In a landmark paper[15] published in 1969, Chauncey Starr[16] discusses public acceptance of risk for voluntary versus involuntary exposure as well as air versus automobile travel and a number of similar comparisons. He concludes that the public is willing to accept "voluntary" risks that are 1,000 times greater than "involuntary" risks. Among other interesting conclusions, Starr notes that, "The social acceptance of risk is directly influenced by the benefits of an activity, as determined by advertising, usefulness, and the number of people participating."

Considering that exposure to radioactive material is not only an involuntary risk but it has additional dread bestowed by the lack of understanding of the cause of harm, the extent that the human body can tolerate radiation, and the fact that terrorist threat is ubiquitous and unpredictable, radioactive materials may be the ultimate weapon of choice.

If it is true radioactive materials are the ultimate terrorist weapon of choice, Starr's conclusions are key to reducing risk. We need to reduce the opportunity of the terrorist to obtain

---

[15] Starr, Chauncey, Social Benefit versus Technological Risk, What is our society willing to pay for safety?, Science, September 1969, Vol. 165, pp. 1232-1238.

[16] Starr, Chauncey, nuclear physicist, and nuclear power engineer. Founder of the Electric Power Research Institute. Former Dean of UCLA School of Engineering. Recognized as the "father" of Risk Analysis/Assessment.

materials, thus preventing an involuntary event from occurring. We must constantly advertise the benefits of radioactive materials to increase the tolerance of the public to low-level radiation and we must inform everyone, including and especially the media, of the true risk. If our physician suspects we could have a cancerous growth on our lungs, no one refrains from a chest x-ray to avoid radiation exposure. We all perceive the potential benefit of having the diagnostic x-ray greatly outweighs the risk. If everyone realized that the amount of (additional) radiation exposure incurred in most terrorist events involving radioactive materials is negligible and does not pose a threat to their health, the fear of these events will greatly diminish, as will the probability of having such an event.

CHAPTER 5 ▨▨▨▨▨▨▨▨▨▨▨▨

How to Use Weapons of Mass Disruption

Sami Kahn stepped off the 176 OCTD bus near the corner of Bristol and Campus Drive. He shrugged his backpack into a more comfortable position and switched his overnight bag to his right hand. Sami headed directly for Ballston Aviation and covered the quarter mile quickly.

"Hi, Sami," said John from behind the counter as Sami entered the door. "Are you ready for your first overnighter?"

"You bet," replied Sami as he rolled his backpack off his shoulder and set it down on the table. "I can't wait to leave. This is why I started taking lessons."

"Do you have a girlfriend in Santa Barbara? I'll bet that's why you are going up for the night."

"You might say that," replied Sami, thoughtfully. He saw John's quizzical reaction to his introspective response and flashed a broad smile to compensate. Then he sat down at the small desk reserved for customers and began filling out his flight plan.

It was half past ten in the morning when Sami filed his flight plan and went through the pre-flight checklist with John. He finally climbed into the plane, got into the seat and fastened the harness. The Cessna 172 started up on the first try and Sami taxied out to the runway. When he was cleared by the tower for takeoff, he pulled out the throttle. When the engine reached 2,500 rpm, he released the brakes and started down the runway.

He was totally consumed with the mechanics of flying until he reached an altitude of three thousand feet and had cleared the high traffic region around John Wayne airport. Sami could see the white crested waves lapping onto the sand in Huntington Beach with the pier jutting out over a quarter mile into the calm Pacific Ocean.

Sami had walked that beach many times in the last ten years and it brought back pleasant memories. His high school years were filled with good times. He was a popular student and he made good grades. He assumed his aptitude for math and science was inherited from his father and uncle. Both were engineers. They had attended college in Pakistan and both got masters degrees when they immigrated to the United States. Sami had always assumed he too would become an engineer.

The big change in Sami's life started when he spent the summer after graduation from high school with his grandparents in Karachi. He got to know his cousins and learn about his roots. It was that summer he realized he was living the life of an infidel. His parents were Muslim in name only and they scarcely ever attended mosque. Sami began to see how badly his father and uncle had been treated in the United States. They were not promoted at their jobs and were paid much less than the other engineers. When they had tried to pray at work, they had been ostracized and soon abandoned the practice and just tried to fit in. His own father had to drive a cab to make ends meet when he first came to America. His uncle worked at a convenience store.

America supposedly has freedom of religion, he reflected, but try to bring in a prayer rug or take a holiday during Ramadan and you quickly learn there is religious freedom for Christians and Jews only.

Sami had always fit in. His dark good looks were attractive to girls. He was often assumed to be Jewish when he was first introduced. Sammy Cohen, not Sami Kohn. It irritated him that he was more easily accepted when people thought he was Jewish and not Muslim. He had heard too many jokes about working at the 7-11 and hated being known as a "Paki".

Sami could see Long Beach harbor below him. Soon he would be in LAX airspace. He knew to avoid the airport and the congestion caused by the big airliners. Today the visibility was excellent. A mild Santa Ana had blown all the pollution out of the Los Angeles basin and he could see the high rises standing tall along the Harbor Freeway. The wind was out of the northeast at about ten to fifteen. *That will work*, he thought.

Sami banked into a sharp ninety-degree turn and headed straight for downtown LA. He knew he was veering from his flight plan, but it was too late for anyone to stop him. He followed the Harbor Freeway north directly toward his targets. Now, the overnight bag in the luggage compartment was his only concern. It had been delivered to his apartment this morning. He didn't have a clue who brought it but he knew what it contained. Sami reached across the cockpit and opened his backpack. He took out his tagiyah and carefully placed it on his head. He unzipped the side pocket of the pack, took out the cell phone, and checked to make sure it was turned on.

The Bank of America building loomed in front of him. It was almost time. Sami pulled out his beads and began to recite his final prayer. Just before the Cessna hit the high rise, Sami punched in the auto dial on his cell phone. The Cessna exploded and airplane parts combined with powered cesium-137 showered down onto Los Angeles.

* * *

Emergency responders raced toward the crash through Los Angeles traffic. The police arrived first, then the fire department. Fragments from the Cessna had hit the Bank of America building, breaking windows. The engine of the Cessna had lodged in an office on the thirtieth floor. Small fires were burning on sidewalks around the building. A thick cloud of smoke drifted west but was soon dissipated by the wind.

Not long after the fire trucks arrived, the Battalion Commander got on the bullhorn and ordered everyone to evacuate the area. High levels of radiation had been detected and all first responders were being pulled back. Soon downtown LA was eerily absent of human life. The office workers were directed to shelter in place until more information became available. Traffic had come to gridlock. Drivers were abandoning their cars in an attempt to leave the area on foot. Every radio station in the LA area had interrupted normal programming. News helicopters were directed to evacuate the area and return to their home airports to be checked for radioactive contamination. The entire downtown area was cordoned off. It would be many days before the offices would reopen.

Every television news channel was now broadcasting the story. As the Los Angeles event unfolded, CNN reported that a truck, believed to be a UPS delivery van, had exploded near Wall Street in downtown New York. Lower Manhattan was completely shut down. In Chicago, an automobile, thought to be a cab, had exploded on Whacker. Michigan Avenue was closed as well as La Salle Street. High radiation levels had been detected at both sites.

As night approached on the west coast, it became obvious a new era of terror had begun. The President was scheduled to address the nation at 9:00 p.m. The Director of the Department of Homeland Security issued a statement that the levels of radiation were not life threatening and urged everyone to stay in their homes. In spite of her advice, a mass exodus continued from the affected cities. Traffic was backed up on all major arteries.

Al Jazeera aired an audio tape reportedly sent by Al Qaeda, claiming responsibility for the attacks and predicting more to come. Fox news network was the first to bring on an expert on nuclear radiation. Dr. Wolf assured the public the explosions were not "atomic bombs". He opined that conventional explosives were used to scatter radioactive material such as can be found in many hospitals. "There is no immediate danger from radiation," he advised.

Internet blogs were filled with conspiracy theories. Bloggers feared additional attacks. They discounted the advice of Homeland Security regarding the danger from radiation. What else would you expect the government to say? Why was everyone wearing hazmat suits if there was no danger? Survivalists immediately began to excitedly discuss their next moves.

*   *   *

The preceding scenario is completely viable. One of the biggest concerns of Homeland Security and law enforcement in general is the homegrown radical. Timothy McVeigh[17] was able to amass a truckload of ammonium nitrate and the explosives to detonate it without arousing suspicion of being a terrorist. Why? Because he looked and sounded just like most of the inhabitants in that part of the United States. He fit into his surroundings. A lone terrorist that does not reveal his plans to anyone else has a very high probability of successfully committing a terrorist act.

---

[17]   Timothy McVeigh was executed on June 11, 2001, for detonating a bomb in front of the Alfred P. Murrah building in Oklahoma City. This explosion claimed the lives of 168 people and injured 450. McVeigh reportedly sought revenge against the federal government for its handling of the Waco Siege of 1993 and other governmental raids as well as disagreement with U.S. foreign policy. This was the deadliest act of terrorism within the Unites States prior to the September 11, 2001, attacks.

The fewer people that are aware of a plot to cause a terrorist act, the more likely they will be successful.

Whether we like it or not, law enforcement relies upon profiling to identify and apprehend criminals. It cannot be otherwise. If law enforcement personnel investigated crimes without regard to sex, religion, age, race, education, economic status, or national origin the cost would be prohibitive and the results would be dismal. Further, law enforcement cannot take action until an actual crime has occurred and been detected. A person cannot be arrested for what they are thinking. Cops know their beat, their territory, and they can normally identify likely suspects very quickly. Even if they do not know who the suspect is, they usually know someone that will know.

The most difficult crimes to solve are those committed at random and by persons not related to the victim. One of the authors (Jones) worked at the Texas Department of Public Safety for over five years and personally witnessed numerous cases from the time the crimes were committed until they were solved. Only in a very few instances was the perpetrator a wild card or anonymous individual. Wives and husbands are killed by their spouse, jealous lovers, business associates, or close relatives. Rival gang members shoot each other. Repeat offenders rob banks. Drug related crimes are done by addicts and pushers. That is why crimes like the Green River Killer[18] serial murders and the infamous Jeffrey Dahmer[19] murders can take many years to solve.

---

[18]   Gary Leon Ridgeway was convicted of the serial murders of women near Renton, Washington. He is believed to have killed at least 71 women. A majority of the killings occurred between 1982 and 1984. He strangled his victims, sometimes using his bare hands and others using a ligature (cord, rope, or wire). He was arrested in November 2001.

[19]   Serial killer and sex offender. Dahmer was indicted on 17 murder charges. His span of killings ranged from June 1978 to July 1991. He was finally arrested in 1991.

They tend to select victims at random and may have no former connection at all with the people they kill.

The homegrown terrorist is particularly dangerous because they appear to be no different than anyone else. They may have become radicalized through their religious beliefs, some real or imagined wrong they have suffered, or even the need to become famous.

It is interesting to compare these horrific events, the Green River attacks, Timothy McVeigh's bombing of the Murrah building, the September 11, 2001, terrorist attacks, and the Sami Khan scenario, and determine what, if anything, they have in common.

Gary Leon Ridgeway, known as the Green River Killer, was apprehended on November 30, 2001. He was linked to the killings by DNA evidence. The majority of his 71 known victims were murdered between 1982 and 1984. Most were prostitutes and were picked randomly off the streets near Renton, Washington. It took almost 20 years for law enforcement to solve this crime. Since the use of DNA in criminal investigations was unknown in the early 1980's, one wonders if Ridgeway would have been apprehended at all had he known leaving one's DNA at the scene of the crime was sufficient to connect him to the event.

The Timothy McVeigh terrorist bombing is, at first glance, completely different. McVeigh was apparently motivated by sociopolitical reasons, not psychopathic, as was Ridgeway. However, from a risk assessment viewpoint, they have several things in common. First, however, it is useful to develop a rational method of estimating the probability of success for a terrorist attack.

Anatomy of a terrorist attack

It is possible to estimate the overall probability of a successful terrorist attack by breaking the attack down into individual steps. The attack is comprised of the following:

Step 1 Obtain the materials necessary for the attack

Step 2 Move the materials to the site of the attack without being apprehended

Step 3 Successfully carry-out the attack

Step 4 Avoid apprehension

In Step 1, the perpetrator(s) must obtain the materials that will be used in the attack without being apprehended and, if possible, without arousing suspicion. Ridgeway could easily obtain his material since he strangled his victims. McVeigh had to amass tons of fertilizer and obtain a truck and ignition materials. McVeigh was able to accomplish this because he did not arouse suspicion. The 9-11 terrorists had to have much more preparation. They took flying lessons. They hijacked commercial planes and held passengers and crew at bay while they flew to the sites of the attacks.

In all cases, the terrorists had the advantage of surprise. No one was sufficiently alarmed by their preparations to report them to law enforcement before the attack. They performed a "first of a kind" attack. (You may argue the Ridgeway event was not unique and had been done many times throughout history, but serial killers are rare and are so difficult to predict *a priori* that the element of surprise is always with the killer.) If one had to assign a probability of success to Step One, it would be almost 100% for each of the four events except for the 9/11 attacks. The amount of preparation and the number of people required for this attack would reduce the probability of success to a lower value. However, the fact it was a "first of a kind" event greatly increased the probability of success.

In Step Two, the perpetrators must move the materials to the site of the attack without being apprehended. In the case of Ridgeway this was relatively easy. The McVeigh attack required renting a truck, loading the materials, and driving to the site.

Here again we can see the great advantage of a "first of a kind" event. The 9/11 attackers were not detected until it was too late to stop them except for Flight 93. However, these terrorists were suicidal and thus were not concerned about escaping (Step Four). In the Sami Khan scenario, he is also suicidal and there is virtually no warning he is intending to crash his plane into the building.

In Step Three, once the terrorist is successful in getting the materials to the site, the attack must be consummated. The bomb must explode, as in the case of the McVeigh event or the Khan scenario. Ridgeway must strangle his victim without her escaping or arousing alarm. The 9/11 terrorists must be able to fly to the targets and ram the aircraft into the buildings. They were totally successful for the Trade Towers, partially successful at the Pentagon, and unsuccessful for Flight 93. However, taken all together, the 9/11 events must be considered highly successful.

Finally, Step Four adds the condition that the perpetrator will attempt to avoid apprehension. In the 9/11 events and the Sami Khan scenario, this is not a consideration. When the terrorist is unconcerned about being apprehended, it changes the dynamic of the entire event. Even if the attack is not suicidal, if the perpetrator is willing to be killed or caught and suffer punishment the probability of success is greatly increased. Robberies, for example, always include a plan for escape. There is no use in doing the crime if you cannot profit by it, assuming your motivation is self-enrichment. The serial killer always attempts to avoid apprehension, presumably to kill again or satisfy some psychological motivation.

To summarize, these criminal events have several things in common that characterize a "successful" terrorist event. First, these events are all unique. They are unexpected and the attack mode is new or at least very rare. Secondly, the possibility of detection is much lower if the terrorist can blend in with their surroundings. The fewer number of people involved, the more likely the event will be successful.

Finally, if the perpetrator is willing to die or be apprehended, the probability of success is greatly increased. The 9/11 event was unique and the terrorists were willing to die to achieve success. The McVeigh event was unique and the terrorists were willing to risk being caught to achieve their goal. The Ridgeway serial killings may have never have been solved if DNA methodology had not been developed. Another famous serial killer case, Jack the Ripper, which happened before modern crime investigation methods were developed, has never been completely resolved.

The authors believe a terrorist attack using nuclear materials is virtually inevitable. Our enemies will eventually resort to using radioactive materials which are a great terrorist tool because of the unnatural, innate fear humans have of them. Such an attack would represent a unique event, one that has not been used previously. Secondly, homegrown terrorists are lurking in our society who are capable of performing such events. Thirdly, the destructive consequences of an event involving radioactive materials could be almost catastrophic and could adversely affect our behavioral patterns.

Finally, materials are accessible that can be used to cause serious consequences. It is only a matter of time until there is an attack on the United States using radioactive materials. We must prepare by preventing radioactive materials from being obtained whenever possible and, if we are unsuccessful in denying materials of mass disruption to our enemies, we must limit the consequences of an attack. This is a battle we cannot afford to lose.

Many countries in the Middle East are currently undergoing significant political upheaval. Algeria, Bahrain, Egypt, Iran, Iraq, Jordan, Kuwait, Lebanon, Libya, Morocco, Oman, Saudi Arabia,

Syria, Tunisia, and Yemen have all been affected.[20] Additionally, the United States has an ongoing conflict in Afghanistan and Iraq and our relations with Pakistan are strained. We, as a nation, have historically supported non-democratic forms of government for the stated purpose of "stabilizing the region". Unfortunately, many of the inhabitants of these countries sympathize with Al Qaeda or some other, mostly Islamic, factions that could be classified as enemies of the Unites States.

A democratically elected government may not produce the leadership we in the United States would choose, had we a choice. Democracy can be a two-edged sword. The ideologue-filled Muslim Brotherhood is Egypt's best organized political group. They could eventually dominate Egyptian politics or at least move Egypt toward an Islamic theocracy. After winning a majority in the Palestinian Legislative Council in 2006, Hamas took, according to Human Rights Watch, "extraordinary steps to control, intimidate, punish, and at times eliminate their internal rivals." Last year, this group charged Hamas with "egregious crimes" for ordering attacks on Israeli civilians.[21] While these Middle-East political upheavals are playing out, we must plan for the worst-case scenario. The United States will continue to be attacked by terrorists, more than likely associated with foreign organizations, but not necessarily non-citizens. The homegrown terrorist could be our greatest enemy.

Council on Foreign Relations noted[22] that between September 11, 2001, and the end of 2009, the United States Government reported forty-six incidents of "domestic radicalization and

---

[20]   http://www.washingtonpost.com/wp-srv/special/world/middle-east-protests/

[21]   http://www.ajc.com/opinion/pro-con-is-muslim-914670.html

[22]   http://www.cfr.org/terrorism/threat-homegrown-islamist-terrorism/p11509.

recruitment to jihadist terrorism" that involved at least 125 people, according to a May 2010 Rand Corporation report. Half the cases involve single individuals, while the rest represent "tiny conspiracies", according to congressional testimony by Brian Michael Jenkins, author of the Rand report. There had been an average of six cases per year since 2001, but that rose to thirteen in 2009.

As of January 2010, all but two people arrested in the last decade for domestic terror connected to radical Islam have been male. Otherwise, at least three recent think tank reports have concluded that suspects follow no definitive ethnic or socioeconomic pattern, being both immigrant and native-born, and ranging in age from 18 to 70. "The only common denominator appears to be a newfound hatred for their native or adopted country, a degree of dangerous malleability, and a religious fervor justifying or legitimizing violence that impels these very impressionable and perhaps easily influenced individuals toward potentially lethal acts of violence," argues a September 2010 paper by the Bipartisan Policy Center.[23]

Given that there are those among us, who look and talk as a "typical" American, it will become more difficult to prevent them from gaining access to and deploying Weapons of Mass Disruption. When these individuals become radicalized, they are extremely dangerous. For example, they can be granted security clearances, become trusted employees with access to radioactive materials, or even become supervisors or managers. Background checks might not reveal their radicalization.

---

[23] Addressing the Terrorist Threat, A report of the Bipartisan Policy Center's National Security Preparedness Group, Peter Bergen and Bruce Hoffman, September 10, 2010.

In the Sami Khan scenario at the beginning of this chapter, there was no reason to suspect him as a terrorist. He was born in the United States, educated here, and, on the surface, appeared to be much the same as anyone else of his age and social strata. Yet, he harbored a grievance that drove him to a suicidal mission. Timothy McVeigh was a former Marine and Bronze Star recipient, yet he was radicalized to the extent that he murdered 168 people in cold blood.

Anwar al-Awlaki is a New Mexico-born radical Muslim cleric accused of recruiting for Al Qaeda. Awlaki has increasingly advocated violent jihad. Sometimes called the Osama bin Laden of the Internet, Awlaki corresponded with Fort Hood-shooter Nidal Hasan, a group in Minnesota responsible for recruiting for al-Shabaab and three of the September 11 hijackers. His lectures were also mentioned by one of the men convicted in the Fort Dix plot, and would-be Times Square bomber Faisal Shahzad. In April 2010, the Obama administration authorized a targeted killing of Awlaki, who is in hiding in Yemen.

The list of radicalized terrorists is growing. Of course, the most dangerous terrorists are the ones that are yet unknown. It is virtually impossible to predict what will be the catalyst that produces a radical terrorist. As countries like France pass laws prohibiting wearing of face coverings (niq-b) and immigrants from Moslem countries are marginalized economically, not to mention the high profile support provided to Israel by the United States; when U.S. citizens decry the construction of a Mosque, simply because it is near the "twin towers" site in New York City; then resentment can be transformed to hatred. Hatred can manifest into terrorist action. These individuals fight what is termed an unsymmetrical war. They are aware that they cannot compete using conventional combat tactics.

The terrorist attack may be the result of a desperate attempt to cause pain and suffering for one's enemy. It may be aggravated by a feeling of hopelessness and impotence in the face of an overwhelming enemy. Whatever the cause, the enemy is at our door and we must find a way to successfully combat them.

CHAPTER 6 ▨▨▨▨▨▨▨▨▨▨▨▨▨

REGULATION OF MIAN MATERIALS

Does anyone regulate the use of radiation or radioactive materials? The answer, of course, is yes. Federal and certain state governments (known as agreement states) currently regulate the use of radiation and radioactive materials. Before we discuss current regulations, it is useful, not to mention interesting, to understand the history of nuclear materials. This will lead into a discussion of how and why regulations were developed as well as emergency preparedness for radiation and radiation sources.

Radiation, and hence, radioactive material, was perhaps the earliest hazard to be regulated. Early work with radiation began in 1895 when Wilhelm Roentgen used an electron beam directed toward a cathode to create "mysterious rays" that penetrated his wife's hand and placed an image of her skeleton on a photographic plate.[24] Antoine Becquerel, a French physicist, became interested in Roentgen's work and began studying fluorescence and phosphorescence. He found that while fluorescence, phosphorescence, and x-rays had many similarities, they also had significant differences. In 1896, Becquerel stored some crystals containing uranium and some photographic

---

[24]   NDT Resource Center: NDT Course Material—Radiography. History of Radiography, online 11/12/2009.

plates together. He found that the plates had been exposed from "invisible emanations" from the crystals. No external energy source was required to initiate the emanations, as was necessary for fluorescence, phosphorescence, and x-rays.[25] However, Becquerel did not pursue investigations into this "discovery of radiation."

During his work, Becquerel had noted that the emanations from uranium caused conductivity in air. Marie and Pierre Curie, working in the Becquerel lab, began researching emanations from various elements to determine their ability to cause conductivity. In 1898, when testing pitchblende, an ore of uranium, they found that it provided 300 times the current of that caused by pure uranium. The Curies concluded that an unknown substance was present in the pitchblende and named it polonium (after Poland, Marie's native country).[26] They coined the phrase "radio-active" to describe the property of emanations from the unknown material.

During the years that followed, x-rays were slowly adapted to medical and industrial uses, while radioactive materials remained in the "research arena." Then in 1945, the United States dropped two atomic bombs in Japan, introducing the "atomic age". The thought that atomic energy could be used to the benefit of mankind, rather than for destruction, permeated throughout society.

The federal government recognized that there were both benefits and pitfalls in the use of radioactive materials, and so the Congress passed the Atomic Energy Act of 1946. The Act established the Atomic Energy Commission (AEC) and placed all control and ownership of radioactive material into the hands

---

[25] Slowiczek, Fran, Ed.D and Pamela M. Peters, Ph.D. Access Excellence Classic Collection—The Discovery Of Radioactivity: The Dawn of the Nuclear Age. Downloaded 11/12/2009.

[26] Ibid

of the federal government. Private use/ownership of radioactive material was not permitted.

Until the 1930's, little consideration was given to radiation protection. In 1934, a committee of representatives from professional societies and x-ray equipment manufacturers recommended a dose limit of 0.1 roentgens per day of whole body exposure. This dose was considered to be a "tolerance dose" that would unlikely cause injury. However, continuing research showed that even small doses could cause changes in reproductive cells and so the tolerance dose began to be less accepted. In 1946, the National Committee on Radiation Protection (NCRP) was formed and it introduced the concept of the "maximum permissible dose". In 1948, the NCRP recommended a maximum permissible dose of 0.3 roentgens per six-day work week. The limit was based on exposure of the "most critical tissue in blood-forming organs, gonads, and lens of the eye."[27]

Congress, in an effort to expand peaceful atomic energy uses, passed the Atomic Energy Act of 1954. The 1954 Act ended the total federal control of radioactive material and required the AEC to encourage research and development of peaceful uses of radioactive material as well as to promulgate regulations that would protect the "public health and safety". This allowed private industry and medical and educational facilities to apply for licenses authorizing the possession and use of radioactive material whether they be for nuclear power production or the more mundane uses of relatively small quantities of radioactive materials. Little progress was made in the development of nuclear power plants until Congress passed the Price Anderson Act in

---

[27] A Short History of Nuclear Regulation, 1946-1999: Nuclear Regulatory Commission, NUREG NUREG/BR-0175, Rev. 1. Downloaded 11/09/2009.

1957. The Act backed insurance companies and allowed them to insure up to $60 million per power plant.

Section 274 of the Atomic Energy Act (AEC), added in 1959, authorized the AEC to enter into an "agreement" with the governor of any state to allow the state to regulate "byproduct materials, source materials, and special nuclear materials"[28] (defined in the Act) in quantities not sufficient to form a "critical mass." The agreement also removed the authority of the AEC in those states, except that the AEC retained authority for certain uses, facilities, and operations. Nuclear power plants, export/ import, and some disposal processes remained under AEC jurisdiction (as did federal facilities). This action did not address radioactive materials that occurred naturally or were produced by accelerators. The states had authority over the latter group.

In the late 1950's, public concern of nuclear matters, even opposition to, began to develop—primarily stimulated by the public's emerging awareness of hazards associated with nuclear power and other uses. While the AEC emphasized stimulation of atomic development, it also was concerned with safety issues and developed regulations that "reflected careful consideration of the best scientific information and judgment available at the time."[29] The AEC believed that "compliance with its regulations would make the chances of a serious accident very small."[30]

The AEC had begun developing relationships with the states in the early 1950's. In 1955, the AEC formed an advisory committee of state officials to advise AEC on federal/state relations. Then in 1962, under Section 274, an agreement

---

28   U.S. NRC, "§ 8.4 Interpretation by the General Counsel: AEC jurisdiction over nuclear facilities and materials under the Atomic Energy Act," (website, accessed December 2010).

29   Ibid. NRC Short History.

30   Ibid.

was signed between the State of Kentucky and the AEC. The agreement allowed the state to regulate the use of most radioactive materials within its borders (the AEC continued regulation of federal uses and certain other types of licenses). Kentucky became the first "Agreement State" (AS). As more and more states signed agreements, the number of AS licenses grew and exceeded the number of AEC licenses in 1971. Adoption of applicable federal radiation control regulations was one of the requirements for a state to sign an agreement with the AEC. There are currently 37 AS and one state has a pending application.[31]

Electric utilities became concerned with the environmental problems caused by the use of coal fired electric plants and the production of electricity by nuclear plants began to look more and more appealing. In the late 1960's, a "reactor boom" was evident as more and more applications were received for larger and larger nuclear plants. While the AEC's nuclear power workload increased tremendously, staff increases could not keep up. Thus, the AEC's attention was directed more towards nuclear plants than towards other uses of radioactive materials. The licensing process became very lengthy and tedious.

Many detractors of the AEC were concerned that it could not both develop and regulate nuclear technology successfully. With the energy crisis created in 1973 and 1974, caused by the Arab oil embargo, Congress was asked by the President to create an agency that could concentrate more on licensing of nuclear power plants. In response, Congress passed the Energy Reorganization Act (ERA) of 1974. The ERA divided the AEC into the Energy Research and Development Administration (ERDA) and the Nuclear Regulatory Commission (NRC).

---

[31] U.S. NRC, "Agreement State Program". (website, accessed December 2010).

During the 1960's and 1970's, many states began developing emergency response plans in the event that natural or manmade disasters might occur. Consequently, the AEC/NRC required the power plant operators to develop emergency response plans that integrated state emergency plans into their procedures. Even though the states did not regulate the nuclear plants, the state radiation control programs became intimately involved in the overall operations of the plants.

Today, the NRC and the AS work together to both regulate the uses of radioactive materials and to develop appropriate radiation safety and control regulations. There are a number of additional organizations that participate in the process. The Federal Bureau of Investigation (FBI), the Environmental Protections Agency (EPA), Health and Human Services Department (HHS), Department of Transportation (DOT), Department of Defense (DOD), Department of Energy (DOE), and the Homeland Security Department (DHS) are principle federal agencies involved in radiation matters, along with the various states with radiation control programs.[32] It should be noted that states without agreements also have radiation regulatory programs which deal with radiation uses not under federal jurisdiction.

Prior to the terror attacks of September 11, 2001, security of radioactive materials was barely functional. For example, a user of a large industrial source might only be required to have a padlock on the storage container and a written procedure that stated "the material could only be handled by authorized person(s)". Radiation protection was the major concern of radiation regulatory organizations. After 9/11, the security requirements were greatly increased and solidified.

---

[32] Ibid.

In 2005, the NRC issued an order requiring the development and implementation of "increased controls" (IC) by licensees (both NRC and AS licensees) possessing certain types and quantities of radioactive material[33]. The requirements included more stringent procedures for allowing access to radioactive materials (such as documented background checks of authorized users) and implementation of security systems capable of initiating a timely armed response from a local law enforcement agency. In 2008, fingerprinting and an FBI background check were added to the requirements.

With the development of stringent radiation protection and security requirements over the years, the question remains: are our current standards adequate to protect the public health and safety from both terror activities and natural/manmade disasters?[34]

So while a government regulatory system has been firmly established, and while stringent controls have been implemented for large sources of radioactive materials, is it enough? The authors contend that it is not! Why? There are simply large gaps left that do not adequately protect other materials.

The International Atomic Energy Commission (IAEA) established 5 categories of radioactive materials.[35] However, only the top 2 categories, Categories 1 & 2, have special security requirements. Category 5 includes very small quantities but Categories 3 & 4, larger quantities, have no special security requirements. Theft, collection, and amassment of these sources could result in a sufficient collection of radioactive materials so as to cause a large area of contamination if used with an IED.

---

[33]   US NRC, "Security Orders and Requirements": http://www.nrc.gov/security/byproduct/orders

[34]   The Physics Hypertextbook—X-Rays, downloaded 11/12/2009.

[35]   IAEA Safety Standards Series No. Rs-G-1.9, "Categorization Of Radioactive Sources", International Atomic Energy Agency, Vienna, 2005.

Further, a radioactively contaminated area of say, 1 sq mile, would be nearly as costly in dollars and time to decontaminate as a similar area that had been contaminated by a source, or sources, 1000 times the quantity. Thus, the terror effect would not be lessened much using smaller sources in lieu of the larger, better protected, ones.

If the terror effect is not greatly dependent on the overall quantity of radioactive materials, it follows that we should enhance security for all radioactive materials above the Category 5 quantities. This could be a voluntary program urged onto possessors (licensees) of the Category 2, 3, and 4, as applicable, radiation sources. What is needed is a simple process whereby licensees can evaluate their security level and, if found wanting, take steps to elevate the security level.[36]

The type of security improvements we need are not simply putting another padlock on a storage container. There are a number of factors to consider when determining what security enhancements might be needed. In virtually all situations, a 24/7 armed guard system is not necessary and would be overly expensive; common sense methods are all that is needed. Both active and passive methods can be employed (a padlock would be a passive method, whereas, an armed guard would be an active method).

Passive methods of securing radiation sources might include (but not be limited to):

---

[36]   The authors have developed such a program, the "Enhanced Security Program", through funding by the Sloan Foundation and sponsorship of the ASME-ITI. It should be available for voluntary use in late 2011.

- Locking the device or container
- Positively securing the container to a structure, make part of structure, or use position in structure (elevated platform, for example)
- Enclosing the container within a lockable steel cage
- Locking the door to room/building
- Placing a fence around use/storage facility
- Installing entrance controls for fences

Active methods of securing radiation sources might include (but not be limited to):
- Establishing a security plan or program
- Provide security training for personnel
- Implement a system of authorizing access (background checks for personnel)
- Install monitoring/alarm systems
- Provide video/audio surveillance
- Provide a guard, perhaps armed
- Provide a method of notifying local law enforcement
- Keep devices/containers under surveillance of authorized personnel
- Perform frequent inspection or inventory (more than required)

Each licensee or possessor of the highest four categories of radioactive material should review their program and, if found to be inadequate, implement any of the above methods to improve or enhance their existing program. Periodic reevaluation should also be part of the security program, particularly if the inventory of radioactive materials changes.

A simple $5 padlock located in the right place at the right time might prevent a potential billion dollar decontamination and recovery exercise.

Another potential gap in the system which might provide radioactive material for terrorists is poorly secured waste radioactive materials. Since the 1970's, "anti-nuke" environmental activists have sought to block all waste disposal facilities. During the time period, it was well known in the nuclear industry that the three national disposal sites would not always be available. Efforts were made to establish radioactive waste disposal sites in other states, but the activists created stumbling blocks rather effectively, mostly through scare tactics and misinformation. Consequently, no new resources have been developed and the three sites became more and more limited as disposal resources.

Licensees with unusable or unneeded sources had to either store their material on their own property, transfer it to someone that could use it (and was licensed), or transfer it to a waste broker. One of the authors (Haygood) worked in the Texas radiation control program for over 30 years and learned of many occasions where stored devices containing radioactive material disappeared. Unneeded devices, such as level gauges, were stored on back lots and essentially forgotten for years. Often, they turned up in scrap metal yards years later, stolen or accidentally disposed, but the licensee did not know that they were missing. Some were even melted in steel recycling plants. (Fortunately, now used steel/metal processing facilities monitor for radiation packages at their entrances). Most of the licensed MIAN facilities store unused and waste radioactive material on-site. Security is often not a major issue for them after a while.

A lack of waste disposal facilities created problems for regulatory agencies. The Texas program impounded many sources of radioactive material over the years. They would be stored in an isotope room in the main health department complex where they would wait for transfer (some were transferred to licensees that could reuse them) or disposal. After a while, however, radiation levels rose to the point that the health department employees were beginning to be threatened with excessive exposures. An external down-hole storage facility had to be engineered and constructed so that the material could be relocated away from personnel. The new location was better for the health of the employees, but was less secure. These were problems many regulatory programs faced. Fortunately, the United States Department of Energy (US DOE) established a program of taking "orphan sources" and disposing of them. This got rid of quite a few sources—relocating them to a far more secure circumstance. But many waste sources today remain poorly secured while awaiting disposal.

To resolve this area of potential terrorist weapons, poorly secured waste radioactive materials, we need to establish good waste disposal facilities that will both safely secure the materials and protect humans and their environment. We then need to encourage all licensees to promptly, and safely, dispose of their unwanted radioactive material.

While it is desirable to improve the security status of all radioactive materials and to dispose of those no longer needed, we cannot move forward very quickly unless the regulatory and local authorities participate. Radiation control agencies, both NRC and AS, need to help licensees identify sources at risk and to find appropriate security resources. The agencies should encourage licensees to improve their security where it is not already mandated by rule or regulation. For the smaller sources, security rulemaking is not necessarily the answer. Circumstances vary considerably and a security method for one licensee may not be viable for another. Encouragement of licensees to use a voluntary self-assessment program of evaluating and improving their own security may be the best solution.

Local law enforcement agencies should be knowledgeable of licensees' radioactive materials use and storage and be prepared to assist in the event of an emergency, especially when involving theft for potential terrorist activities. Licensees usually have contacted fire departments to brief them on the hazards located on-site. Now, they should be encouraged to contact local police and sheriff departments and discuss security issues. Radiation control agencies could assist in this process.

Suppose now that a terrorist or terrorist group successfully acquires some radioactive material. Suppose further that they have enough material to cause a very serious, perhaps fatal, exposure to a person who is present within 2 feet of the source for 20 or more minutes. Since the only way to detect or find such a source is by using a radiation detection instrument, it would be undiscoverable for many months—perhaps never. Now if that source were to be placed in a seat (hidden from view) on a public transportation system, where individuals sit for twenty or more minutes, then a very large number of individuals would be exposed. After a mysterious illness with unknown cause developed, the terrorist only needs to report the source and say, "By the way, there are more . . ." to create a very large panic.

How can we protect against such a heinous crime?

One possibility is to place radiation monitoring devices at key locations whereby all of the vehicles of a public transport system would be checked daily. Or a trained person could be assigned to periodically survey all of the vehicles. Each municipality should take into consideration this possibility and determine the best recourse for its area of responsibility. Citizens should be sufficiently informed, and aware of their surroundings, to report suspicious behavior.

Such an attack may not be limited to public transport systems. Any public place where humans spend a great deal of time could be targeted. Public libraries, theaters, even sports arenas could easily be targeted. Major events, such as the Super Bowl in Dallas in 2011, are well covered. But there are many lesser events, attended by thousands, that could be eligible for attack.

CHAPTER 7

SMUGGLING MIAN MATERIALS INTO THE UNITED STATES

In addition to the estimated 21,000 MIAN sites that use or store radioactive materials in the United States, literally millions of radioactive sources are distributed worldwide. Hundreds of thousands of locations possess this material in varying quantities and sizes which is currently being used, stored, and produced. In the United States alone, approximately 2 million licensed sealed sources are in use.[37] While efforts are ongoing to reduce the number of sources and account for "orphaned" and unused materials, it is clear that there is more than enough radioactive material available, worldwide, for terrorist purposes.

Not only do we need to protect domestic sites, we must guard against importing terrorist materials from abroad. The ports of Los Angeles and Long Beach alone handle approximately 14 million twenty-foot-equivalent shipping containers per year. Even if these containers are screened using sensitive detectors, there is always the possibility of exploding the container itself, in effect, a self-contained dirty bomb, before or during screening.

---

[37] General Accounting Office. (2003) Nuclear Security: Federal and State Action Needed to Improve Security of Sealed Radioactive Sources. Available at http://www.gao.gov/new.items/d03804.pdf

The Department of Justice (DOJ) estimates[38] that several thousand tons of illegal drugs are smuggled into the United States annually. There are unique smuggling and transportation methods associated with each drug type. Drug seizure data and law enforcement reporting indicate that overland smuggling and subsequent transportation by vehicle exceed all other methods combined. DOJ provides the following breakdown for common overland smuggling methods.

Mexican drug trafficking organizations (DTO) dominate the transportation of illicit drugs across the Southwest Border. They typically use commercial trucks and private and rental vehicles to smuggle cocaine, marijuana, methamphetamine, and heroin through the 25 land ports of entry (POE) as well as through vast areas of desert and mountainous terrain between POE. Asian traffickers, outlaw motorcycle gangs (OMG), and Indo-Canadian drug traffickers transport significant quantities of high-potency marijuana and MDMA (3, 4-methylenedioxymethamphetamine-known as Ecstasy) into the United States across the U.S.—Canada border. Commercial trucks, private and rental vehicles are used to transport these drugs through more than 100 land POEs. They also use all-terrain vehicles (ATV), aircraft, maritime vessels, and couriers on foot to smuggle drugs through vast areas between POEs.

It must be assumed that terrorist organizations are well aware of how porous our borders are and our lack of resources to patrol them. The sheer volume of drug trafficking that goes undetected bears witness to our inability to prevent smuggling of radioactive materials into the United States. While it is acknowledged that monitoring equipment located at POE's is likely to detect incoming radioactive material, the plethora of routes across our

---

[38]   http://www.justice.gov/ndic/pubs38/38661/movement.htm

borders provides ample opportunity for the terrorist to import radioactive materials undetected. Would it be unreasonable to assume that Mexican DTO's might be amenable to smuggling radioactive materials and/or explosives for terrorist groups for compensation, monetary or otherwise? The DTO's apparently have a great deal of experience and success in smuggling operations and, therefore, would have a good chance of successfully getting these materials into the U.S.

In addition to the material available in the United States, the IAEA reported in 2002 that "the radioactive materials needed to build a 'dirty bomb' can be found in almost any country in the world, and more than 100 countries may have inadequate control and monitoring programs necessary to prevent or even detect the theft of these materials."[39] They further state that "orphaned" radioactive sources—a term utilized by nuclear regulators to denote radioactive sources that are outside official regulatory control—are a widespread phenomenon in the Newly Independent States (NIS) of the former USSR. Even the United States Nuclear Regulatory Commission reports that United States companies have lost track of nearly 1,500 radioactive sources within the country since 1996, and more than half were never recovered. A European Union (EU) study estimated that every year up to about 70 sources are lost from regulatory control in the EU. A recent European Commission report estimated that about 30,000 disused sources in the EU that are held in local storage at the users' premises are at risk of being lost from regulatory control."

Since the 1970's, some environmental groups put up numerous roadblocks when efforts were made to establish radioactive waste disposal resources. Knowing full well that the three (3) existing

---

[39] http://www.iaea.org/newscenter/pressreleases/2002/prn0209.shtml

sites in the U.S. would eventually reach a point where they could not accept additional wastes, these groups fought hard to prevent adding additional disposal sites in other states. Consequently, the disposal costs crept steadily upward and companies with unusable sources simply stored devices containing radioactive material in their general storage areas where they were essentially ignored thereafter. A number of these sources were later discovered to be missing. Some were found at scrap metal processing facilities while others went through processing and were melted into steel. Many were never found again. If taken by terrorists, these sources would probably go undetected.

Though there has been significant progress since 2002 to recover material and prevent further loss, the fact remains that significant amounts of radioactive materials, certainly enough for terrorist purposes, remains at large. While we have made significant progress in locating "lost" material and increasing security, we must assume our enemies have also become more sophisticated in understanding how to obtain, transport, and deploy these materials. We have gained ground in many technical areas; however, we may have lost ground in others. The most notable example, perhaps, is our relationship with countries dominated by the Muslim religion. The possibility of smuggling radioactive material into the United States is very real. Rogue nations are producing these materials and there is much unaccounted for material. If such material can be obtained from foreign sources without detection, the probability of successfully deploying it is greatly increased.

CHAPTER 8

Other Ways to Terrorize with Radiation

In previous chapters, we have presented scenarios to illustrate how radionuclides can be obtained and deployed. They mainly concern the use of MIAN materials as Radioactive Dispersal Devices (RDD). While we believe these events are feasible, the scenarios are fictitious. The story of Alexander Litvinenko is, if anything, stranger than fiction. Litvinenko was murdered using alpha radiation as the murder weapon. The material was not administered using an explosive device, but rather given to him in a cup of tea.

Alexander Litvinenko was born in 1962 in the Russian city of Voronezh. He attended secondary school there and apparently was recognized early on as having a talent for learning languages and possessed higher than average intelligence. Following graduation, he was drafted into the Ministry of Internal Affairs as a Private. After only a year of service, he attended the Kirov Higher Command School in Vladikavkaz, Russia. When he graduated in 1985, Litvinenko became a platoon commander in the Dzerzhinsky Division of the Soviet Ministry of Internal Affairs. In 1986, he became an informant when he was recruited by a section of the Russian KGB. In 1988, he was officially transferred to the Third Chief Directorate of the KGB, Military Counter Intelligence. Later that year, at the age of only twenty-six, he became an operational officer; he served in KGB military counterintelligence until 1991.

Litvinenko was clearly a highly intelligent and ambitious man. In 1991, he was soon promoted to the Central Staff of the Federal Counterintelligence Service, specializing in counter-terrorist activities and infiltration of organized crime. He won several awards and commendations for his service. He also saw active service in many of the so-called "hot spots" of the former USSR and Russia, where he continued to distinguish himself. Although he was often accused of being a spy, throughout his career he was not an "intelligence agent" and did not deal with secrets beyond information on operations against organized criminal groups.

Litvinenko met Boris Berezovsky in 1994 when he took part in investigations into an assassination attempt on the oligarch. He later began to moonlight for Berezovsky where he was responsible for the oligarch's security. The moonlighting by Litvinenko and other security services personnel was illegal, but the State somewhat tolerated it in order to retain personnel who were at the time underpaid. Thus, Litvinenko's moonlighting for the controversial businessman was not investigated, but often investigations in Russia were selective and usually targeted only at those who had stepped out of line.

In 1997, Litvinenko was promoted to the FSB Directorate of Analysis and Suppression of Criminal Groups, with the title of senior operational officer and deputy head of the Seventh Section. According to Dimitri Simes, the Directorate was viewed as much as a part of organized crime as it was of law enforcement. According to Litvinenko's widow, during his tenure of employment in the FSB he discovered numerous connections between top brass of Russian law enforcement agencies and Russian mafia groups, which he detailed in a memorandum to Boris Yeltsin. Berezovsky arranged a meeting for him with FSB Director and deputy directors to discuss the alleged corruption problems. Since nothing resulted from this meeting, Litvinenko concluded that the entire system was corrupt.

In 1998, Berezovsky wrote an open letter to Putin in which he accused Yevgeny Khokholkov[40] and his deputies of ordering the oligarch's assassination. On November 17, 1998, Litvinenko and four other officers, all of whom were in the employ of both the FSB in the Directorate of Analysis and Suppression of Criminal Groups and of Boris Berezovsky on a part-time basis, appeared together in a press conference at the Russian news agency Interfax, at which they repeated the allegation made by Berezovsky four days previous, but offered no evidence to support the accusations. They also claimed they were ordered to kill Mikhail Trepashkin, who was also present at the press conference, and to kidnap a brother of the businessman Umar Dzhabrailov. After holding the press conference, Litvinenko was dismissed from the FSB. Vladimir Putin, former president of the Russian Federation and currently Prime Minister, reportedly said later in an interview that he personally ordered the dismissal of Litvinenko.

Litvinenko was subsequently arrested twice on charges which were dropped after he had spent time in Moscow prisons. In 1999, he was arrested on charges of abusing duties. He was released a month later after signing a written undertaking not to leave the country. Litvinenko reportedly believed that Putin was behind his arrest. In October 2000, in violation of an order not to leave Moscow, Litvinenko and his family travelled to Turkey, possibly via the Ukraine. While in Turkey, Litvinenko applied for asylum at the United States Embassy in Ankara, but his application was denied. With the help of Alexander Goldfarb[41], Litvinenko

---

[40] Director of the Directorate of Analysis and Suppression of Criminal Groups.

[41] Alexander Davidovich Goldfarb, was born in 1947 in Moscow, He is a microbiologist, activist, and author.

bought airline tickets for the Istanbul-London-Moscow flight, and asked for political asylum at Heathrow Airport during the transit stop on November 1, 2000.

Political asylum was granted on May 14, 2001, not because of his knowledge on intelligence matters, but rather on humanitarian grounds. While in London, he became a journalist for the separatist Chechen press and a controversial author, and also joined Berezovsky in campaigning against Putin's government. In October 2006, he became a naturalized British citizen with residence in Whitehaven. Controversy continued to surround Litvinenko. He was accused of working for the British Intelligence agency, MI6, for a reported salary of £2,000 per month. He reportedly was also preparing to engage in a series of blackmail attempts in which he would agree not to publish incriminating information regarding Russian oligarchs and political officials in the Kremlin. Apparently, his access to FSB materials was to become a business model to exploit as a way of supporting himself and his family. His actions resulted in a conviction in absentia in Russia, which carried a three and one half year jail sentence.

On November 1, 2006, Litvinenko suddenly fell ill and was hospitalized. His illness was later attributed to poisoning with the radionuclide polonium-210 (Po-210). (Information about Po-210 can be found in Appendix 3.)

The story of Alexander Litvinenko is particularly relevant to understanding the dangers of radionuclides. This material is an excellent choice for assassinations as well as wholesale murder. Only a miniscule amount is necessary to kill a human. Even the small amount found in the Litvinenko autopsy could have killed 200 people. If properly distributed, an ounce could kill more than one million individuals. This amount can be sent in the U.S. mail for less than fifty cents.

Since Po-210 emits only alpha particles, it is very difficult to detect, a feature that recommends the use of Po-210 since it can be carried through airport detection equipment without triggering an alarm. Alpha particles are stopped by a sheet of paper or a plastic medicine container, and even in a plastic baggie used to contain liquids when we pass through security at airports. It can be heated and cooled without reducing its potential for damage. Thus, it could be baked in bread, served in fried potatoes or packaged in ice cream. As Mr. Litvinenko learned, it can be served at English High Tea as well. Further, Po-210 creates symptoms that do not suggest that the victims are poisoned for days, allowing ample time to escape.

It does not take much imagination to speculate how this particularly dangerous material could be used to cause terrible consequences. Unlike an RDD, this radionuclide could result in massive numbers of fatalities. Used as a terrorist weapon, it is indiscriminate about its victims. Everyone that consumes food or drink containing Po-210 would be equally at risk including men, women, and children. As soon as is it is ingested, it begins to destroy the functions of the body. The alpha particles that are emitted in great quantity are not energetic enough to penetrate even a piece of paper, but they will enter our cells and destroy their function.

Once ingested, all of the decay events will be absorbed by cell tissue. Unlike RDD devices, which scatter materials and cause contamination of physical places, which can be avoided and decontaminated, ingestion guarantees that every single alpha particle emitted will strike a target. Eventually, as cells die and are not replaced, bodily functions will stop and death will surely occur. There is no antidote to reverse the effects of Po-210 poisoning; once you have ingested it and it is in your system, it is just a matter of time until it completes its work. To more fully understand how radiation exposure causes sickness and death, consider the following discussion of the different types of particles emitted by radioactive materials.

There are four (4) principle forms of radiation that need be considered for health effects due to exposure: alpha, beta, and neutron particles, and gamma rays. X-rays are pretty much the same as gamma rays, so we can lump them together.

Alpha particles are large particles that cannot travel very far through non-vacuum conditions; in fact, they are most hazardous when they are emitted from an atom that is located within tissue within a living cell. As a large particle, they have a high probability of interacting with just about anything they encounter. They also have a lot of energy that they can impart to whatever they encounter. Typically, when produced in a cell, they will have several interactions and give up their energy to a number of components of the cell. Many ions can be created within the cell. The presence of the ions creates a variety of effects ranging from reparable damage to damage so severe that it results in cell death. In between these extremes lies serious damage to the cell that does not result in cell death. In this case, cells with DNA damage can carry the damage on through subsequent cell divisions. The end result, then, can be no harm to the cells, organ, or organism; or serious damage to a cell that results in either a malfunctioning organ (damage carried on through future cell divisions) or death to the organ and/or organism. If the organism happens to be a human, we become very concerned.

So how would isotopes that emit alphas wind up in our cells? In most cases, the radioactive atoms are adhered to, and carried by, a non-radioactive particle. The pathways available to the particles are through ingestion (digestive tract), inhalation (breathed in), transpired through the skin (this would be rare), or through cuts and abrasions in the skin including punctures.

Isotopes that are ingested go through the human system according to their chemistry. Some will be processed in the same manner as foods and carried by blood to individual cells. Some will not be digestible and will eventually be processed through and out of the digestive tract.

In most cases, isotopes that are inhaled are attached to particles suspended in the air. These particles are filtered by the respiratory tract. Some particles are breathed in and out without attaching to anything, some are filtered out in the upper tract (sinuses, throat, etc.), and some by the cilia and tissues in the bronchia prior to reaching the lungs. The filtered particles are generally carried by the respiratory tract tissues to and "dumped" into the digestive tract where "things" (foreign materials and waste) are processed out of the body. Thus, an inhalation hazard can also be, in part, a digestion hazard.

Some of the particles that get into the blood stream and into tissues might be filtered out and placed in the lymphatic system, which can slowly remove the material from the body.

Not all particles carrying isotopes, or that are isotopes, are necessarily removed from the body. For example, a radioactive calcium atom would be treated just like a non-radioactive one and would probably wind up in the bones or teeth. In addition, atoms of some elements are treated in the same manner as atoms of other elements that the body needs and processes. An atom of radium-226, a particularly insidious radioactive material, is chemically similar to calcium and would be processed in a similar manner as a calcium atom.

So how do we guard against terrorist actions that could cause ingestion or inhalation? A major first step would be to guard against deliberate introduction of alpha emitting isotopes into our food, water, and air-processing systems. Reasonable security systems should be established for our food source processing. Companies should be aware of their workers' backgrounds. Background checks are required for jobs that involve handling of radioactive materials that are considered "dangerous", but not for most assembly line workers. Further, there is strong resistance on the part of employers, as well as employees, to in-depth investigations, which can result in privacy issues. Even checking the legality of employees with respect to immigration status has met with resistance in the workplace.

Simple radiation detection systems should be set up at the packaging points. This needs to be done for large systems, not the small ones. A terrorist attack could result in very severe consequences if directed against a large company with an extensive distribution network. This type of event could result in many deaths and serious injuries, not to mention the possibly catastrophic financial effect on the target firm and all similar business in this economic sector. Attacking a small firm with limited product distribution would not result in as many casualties, but the psychological effects could still be overwhelming. Further, larger companies have more resources for setting up protective systems.

Introduction of an alpha emitter, such as Po-210, to a popular brand of cereal and the subsequent distribution throughout the United States would be hard to prevent or even discover. Due to the alpha's limited range and penetrability, "pure" alpha emitting radioactive material must be discovered before packaging. Alpha emitting radioactive material that emits other radiations can be detected downstream in the production process. For example, the alpha emitting americium-241 (Am-241) isotope also emits a rather weak, but detectable, gamma. So Am-241 contaminants could probably be detected after packaging, provided that production and shipping processes are monitored.

Given that such materials are extremely hard to detect and are deadly when ingested, how do we protect ourselves from this type of attack? The best answer is to prevent them from falling into the hands of terrorists. Po-210 is a very scarce material. It also has a relatively short half-life of only 138 days and decays into a stable isotope of lead. Thus, it is reduced to one-eighth of its original activity in about eighteen months after it is produced. This means that this material cannot be obtained and held for years before deploying it; it "spoils" quite rapidly.

The principal uses of Po-210 are as a static eliminator or air ionizer. The positively charged alpha particles are useful for eliminating negative charge, such as can develop on photographic film. Today's static eliminators offer either Po-210 or Am-241, but many non-radiation devices and techniques have been developed and are also offered. Some of these products can be readily purchased over the internet[42] and disassembled to obtain the Po-210. While it would require a relatively large number of such devices to accumulate the material, the amount of Polonium required to cause terror is small.

---

[42]   See Amstat Industries, Inc. http://www.amstat.com/solutions/nuclear/bars.
        html

CHAPTER 9 ▪▪▪▪▪ ▪ ▪ ▪ ▪ ▪ ▪ ▪ ▪ ▪ ▪ ▪

WHY DON'T WE ELIMINATE MIAN MATERIALS?

Mahmaud looked at the alarm clock for the fourth time in the last five minutes. It was finally almost time to get up. He shut off the alarm and walked to the bathroom. As he shaved for the last time, he regretted having to give up his beard. It was a sacrifice, but necessary if you wanted to work in America without arousing suspicion. *It will grow back soon,* he thought. *I can't wait to see the family again. They haven't seen me without a beard since I was about sixteen. Only a few more days now, if everything goes right.*

Mahmaud pulled on faded jeans and a Dallas Cowboy sweatshirt. He picked up a soft leather suitcase as he looked around the sparsely furnished room. *Nothing left behind,* he concluded. He had checked the contents of his luggage a dozen times last night, yet he had to overcome the urge to go through it once more.

He dialed the combination to the lock and pulled up the garage door. Opening the trunk of his old Honda, he stashed his suitcase and then walked back to the open door and looked both ways along the rows of garages in the cheap apartment complex. *No one up yet. Good.* He quickly traversed the garage, unlocked, and opened the Army surplus footlockers in front of the Honda. Stooping down, Mahmaud removed four AK-47 automatic rifles and placed them on the floor of the garage. He took five canvas bags out of the other footlocker and added an AK-47 to four of them, zipped, and moved them to the trunk of the Honda. He checked the contents of the last one once again and put it behind the seat.

He got into the car and turned the key. The motor started and he was relieved. *I don't need a problem this morning,* he thought. Mahmaud backed out, closed, and locked the garage door and drove away, just like every other day. As he drove along the interstate, he tuned the radio to the traffic report. *About normal. Good. One less worry.*

He took the turnout to the rest stop and drove slowly by the restrooms. He spotted the minivan parked in the last space, parked next to it, and turned off his engine. A young man in a baseball cap approached and they looked at each other warily. "I am Latife Mar . . ."

Mahmaud held up his hand and interjected, "Hold it! We use first names only. Today we are going to be presidents. You are George. You can call me Manny. They already know me at the plant."

"Sorry." he responded. "Khushtar and Sarab are in the truck," he added.

"Today, they are Ronald and Jimmy. Got it?"

"Got it. We are ready."

"All right. Let's get going. We have to be there by nine sharp," replied Mahmaud. "I've got something for you. Take three bags," he said, nodding toward the trunk. "Be careful when you take them out. Extra ammo is in the bags."

"We're ready," reported "George" as he closed the sliding door to the minivan.

"Follow me," said Mahmaud as he started the Honda and backed out. They left the rest stop and pulled back onto the interstate.

As the vehicles approached a large concrete building located on about 30 acres of fenced land Mahmaud turned on his emergency flashers briefly. The minivan flashed his headlights and pulled off onto the berm. In the rear view mirror, Mahmaud saw Latife exit the van and raise the hood as if he was having engine problems. The Honda continued into the long driveway and stopped at the guard station.

"Morning, Fred," said Mahmaud as he flashed his ID.

"Morning, Manny. Good to see you. Habib is already here. He got here about ten minutes ago. Are you guys ready for the source change out? I don't envy you."

"It's not that bad, Fred. We'll get it done. We're not replacing today, just rearranging. This is a piece of cake."

"You are welcome to it," replied Fred as he handed the temporary badge to Latife. "Are you going to be here all day?"

"Most of the day, Fred," said Mahmaud. "If we're lucky we might get out a little early today. Do me a favor. Call me when the RadTechs get here. You have my cell number?"

"Sure Manny. I'll give you a call as soon as they arrive."

Mahmaud steered the Honda slowly up the drive to the parking lot and parked one slot away from a large white heavy-duty delivery van. Mahmaud recognized Habib waiting in the driver's seat. He nodded and gestured for Habib to follow him. They removed the two remaining canvas bags from the trunk of the Honda and walked up to the main door. The parking lot and building were deserted; the rest of the employees enjoyed a holiday when there was source work to be done.

Mahmaud punched in his code and heard the door unlock. They carried their bags into the lobby. Normally a security guard would check their IDs but today the building was deserted except for external security and the sterilizer unit operator. They moved quickly down the hall to the physics suite and entered a vacant office. They donned bulletproof vests, white sterile overalls, and put on tactical radio headsets.

"Com check. This is one," said Mahmaud. He listened as four distinct voices responded in turn. "A-Okay. We go at nine sharp. Two minutes until show time. Put on your gloves. We don't want to leave any prints."

At exactly nine o'clock, the minivan pulled back onto the highway and proceeded around the site to a back gate. The passenger efficiently cut the lock on the gate and the minivan pulled through. He placed a new lock on the gate, climbed back into the vehicle, and they drove along the gravel road to a maintenance door. Three men got out, grabbed their bags, and stepped up the stairs to the service door.

Mahmaud and Habib approached the video surveillance room. Mahmaud knocked at the door and the guard, recognizing them, automatically pressed the lock release button.

"Hey, Manny, you're not supposed to come in here. What do you need?"

Mahmaud pulled the AK-47 from behind his back and said, "Sorry Jim, but I have no time for pleasantries."

The stunned guard sat motionless. Habib rushed in and handcuffed him.

"Take him to the men's room and cuff him to the plumbing," Mahmaud barked. "Be quiet. Do as I say and you might live through this, Jim," said Mahmaud sternly.

Mahmaud activated his radio and calmly stated, "Guard secured. Proceed."

He studied the board for a moment and then pressed the latch release for the back access door. Latife, Khushtar, and Sarab heard the lock click open; they entered and proceeded to the video surveillance room.

Habib returned to the delivery van, started it, drove behind the main building to the loading dock, and backed up. Habib pressed the access buzzer and waited. When he heard the lock thud open, he opened the rear doors of the van and unloaded a heavy-duty cart.

Mahmaud and Latife walked quickly to the sterilizer operator station. One look at the AK-47s convinced the operator.

"Put him in the stall next to Jim. Be sure to cuff him to something substantial," said Mahmaud as he turned to the control panel.

Mahmaud carefully checked the irradiator control panel. A mistake now could be fatal. The Co-60 racks were definitely down in the shielding water pool. He turned the control key to the lock position, removed it, and slipped it into his pocket.

Mahmaud returned to the surveillance room to find everyone gathered there.

"OK, men. We have at least eight hours to do this. Four hours would be better. Ronald, keep a sharp lookout for the RadTech guys. Fred is supposed to call me, but I can't count on him. The rest of you come with me."

Khushtar remained in the surveillance room to watch the security monitors. Mahmaud led the others to the sterilization room. He walked over to the pool and looked down. It was hard to believe he was looking through thirty feet of water. He could see every detail on the bottom.

Sarab and Riyad pushed the heavy cart to within five feet of poolside. They removed the canvas cover to revealed four cylindrical canisters. They removed the end caps; the cross section showed radiation shielding around aluminum central tubes. There was plenty of shielding to limit the dose until they got the canisters to the truck. The racks in the truck contained additional shielding that, with any luck, would pass through roadside radiation detectors.

Not a bad design, thought Mahmaud. *I spent many years learning how to do this. Fifteen pellets in each container, four containers. That makes sixty Co-60 pellets. Our guys can do a lot of damage with sixty of these little fellows.*

Mahmaud jumped when his cell phone rang. He saw it was Fred.

"Hi, Fred. Thanks for the call. Yes, we will meet them at the door. Thanks Fred."

Mahmaud spoke into his radio, "George and you. What's your name? Yes, yes. Ronald. Go to the front door and greet our visitors. Be sure to take their cell phones. Just strip their pockets. Handcuff them and put them in with the others. If you run out of stalls, use the women's. Hurry! Come back here as soon as you're done. The faster we finish the better."

Mahmaud pulled a long canvas bag from the cart. He removed six five-foot long aluminum tubes and screwed them together. At one end of the assembled pole was a cutting wheel with a diamond blade powered by a small DC motor. The watertight power cord extended the length of the pole. Mahmaud taped the cord to the pole as he lowered the cutting wheel to the bottom of the pool.

"Habib, bring the cart closer," he ordered. "Help me lower this."

They strained to lift the short hollow cylinder and set it next to the side of the pool. Attaching a sturdy steel chain to the cylinder, they slowly lowered it to the bottom of the pool.

Mahmaud expertly scanned the row of cobalt-60 racks positioned along the pool. Seeing the one he wanted, he went to the end of the pool and grasped a rack-manipulating tool. Pulling it through the transparent pool water, he positioned it carefully and released the rack and rack-top. He now had access to the pencils containing the cobalt-60 pellets. He went to the end of the pool again and retrieved a pencil-manipulating tool. Using this tool, he pulled one pencil from the rack and set it to the side. As he was finishing, he looked up to see Khushtar and Sarab returning.

"The RadTech reps are cuffed," they reported.

"Good. Now we have everything under control. George, I want you to check on our guests every few minutes. We don't want them to get too lonesome in the bathroom and maybe get into mischief. The rest of you get ready for some action. We are about to liberate some of these little guys."

Mahmaud reached with the cutting tool to the bottom of the long thin cylinder, known as a pencil, and cut off the bottom. The stainless steel rod was tough but the diamond-cutting wheel made short work of it. Using the tool, he shook the pencil. Nothing happened.

This was the unknown part. Everything else was predictable and controllable. He thought, *How tight was the fit between the pellets and the cylinder? Did the saw leave a ragged edge on the tube? How much force would it take to get them out?*

Mahmaud pulled the cutting tool up to the top of the pencil and cut the top off. He lifted the pencil again and shook it. Several pellets fell to the bottom of the pool. *Good. Good.*

Mahmaud went to the cart and removed another set of thin rods from the long canvas bag and screwed them together. *Plan B*, he mused. *I hope this works because there's no plan C.*

He went back to the pool and, with Latif holding the pencil rod manipulator; Mahmaud inserted the long thin rod into the open end of the pencil tube and pushed the remaining pellets out of the tube. They fell free and rolled around the bottom of the pool.

Mahmaud used a grasping tool to pick up the pellets one by one and place them in the short, thick walled container, closed the cylinder cap, and began to hoist it up to the surface. Latife, seeing him struggle, grabbed hold of the chain. Together they pulled the cylinder to the surface and lifted it atop the waiting shielded containers. Mahmaud pulled a lever at the base of the transfer cylinder and the pellets fell into the shipping container.

"It works, men. We have money in the bank," said Mahmaud, trying not to sound surprised. "Now it is just a matter of time until we have everything we came here for."

Working under water made for slow going, but by afternoon, they had loaded each of the four cylinders with 15 pellets. As the cylinders were filled, they were transported to the waiting van. Numerous stray pellets were scattered around the pool bottom by the time they were finished, but that was part of the plan.

"Habib, take George with you and go to the front gate. Bring back the guard," ordered Mahmaud. "Put him in with the rest of them. Fred was scheduled to leave over an hour ago and this new guy doesn't get off until midnight. By the time the next guard gets here, we'll be long gone. Lock down the guardhouse, turn out the lights, and close the gate. Unless someone knows there's always supposed to be a guard there, they'll think the whole place is shut down. I have a little more damage to do here."

Mahmaud retrieved the last of the canvas bags and removed his prized creation. He had made it himself and tested it several times using firecrackers. He set the trigger next to the pool and lowered the waterproof explosive into the water using the lead wires. He taped the trigger to the guardrail and opened up the cell phone on top of it. The phone was showing four bars. The cell service was great here. *That is one good thing about America,* he thought. The underwater explosion would mangle the pencils and probably release enough radiation to keep everyone at bay for long enough. The pressure pulse might even blow a hole in the pool wall and let the shielding water drain out. That would be too much to ask.

Mahmaud returned to his men. "Let's move," he commanded. "Our work is almost done. Don't leave anything behind."

As the three vehicles exited the rear gate, the Honda headed toward the international airport via the Interstate. The minivan turned off onto a side road a mile away and soon was lost in the wooded countryside. The delivery van stuck to back roads and headed for the state line. It would make several deliveries before it was finished giving up its load. Its destinations included a self-storage locker, two small businesses, and a farmhouse.

*　　*　　*

It seemed like an eternity before the Boeing 777 was finally boarded. Mahmaud placed his carry-on in the overhead bin. He settled himself in his seat and listened intently as the flight attendant encouraged the passengers to finish stowing their gear and take their seats. When the cabin door was finally closed, Mahmaud made one last call from his cell phone.

*　　*　　*

In the preceding scenario, a sterilization irradiation facility was attacked to obtain Co-60 for use by other terrorists. Conventional wisdom has been that the radioactive material in such facilities cannot be taken, as it is so highly radioactive that an attempt to remove it would be fatal to the perpetrators. The authors have presented what we believe is a scenario that could be actually be accomplished. One of the weaknesses of the facility is the belief that it is secure. This mindset will greatly increase the probability of success for the terrorists.

An irradiation facility as described above contains thousands of Curies. This makes it a prime target for those wanting to obtain the material. These facilities typically operate around the clock and may run seven days a week. A sketch of a typical facility follows:

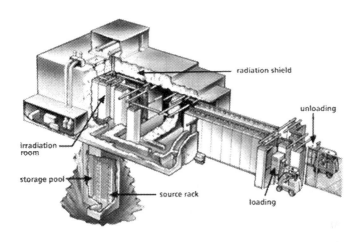

Materials to be sterilized or preserved are loaded onto conveyers (or conveyor belts) similar to the baggage-handling conveyers at an airport. The conveyers take the product from the loading area, through a radiation shield, and into the irradiation room. The material stays in the room, usually controlled by the speed of the moving conveyer belt, for long enough for the radiation to kill all bacteria in the product. The product then is conveyed out of the irradiation room, past the shield, removed from the conveyer, and shipped to the end user. None of the material that passed through the irradiator is radioactive! The advantage to this process over conventional heat sterilization is that the items are sealed in the packaging and then sterilized, whereas heat sterilization requires package sealing after treatment, thereby giving opportunity for organisms to be reintroduced to the items. Primarily, medical supplies and food are the items subject to sterilization. They will neither be harmed, altered nor will they become radioactive.

The radioactive material used in the facility, called sources or radiation sources, is shielded by a storage pool when not in use. Water is a good shielding material and when technicians need to access the irradiation room, they lower the radioactive material into the pool thereby allowing them access. The principal isotope used as the source of radiation is cobalt-60 (Co-60). This material is produced in Canada and is manufactured into small metallic pellets. The pellets are encapsulated in stainless steel cylinders about one-half inch in diameter and up to 10 feet long. These cylinders are placed into racks that can be raised out of the water. When a storage rack is lifted out of the pool, the irradiation room is subjected to extremely high radiation levels, thousands of rads per minute. Human exposure to this radiation field is fatal in only a few minutes.

When the sources require rearrangement, which happens because the "pencils" are of different age and thus they lose "power" due to radioactive decay as they get older, they are rearranged so that the radiation field used to sterilize the products is more uniform. There are also shutdowns when some of the older pencils (which have reduced activity due to degeneration according to the half-life schedule discussed elsewhere in this book) are replaced by "new" ones. The material for all irradiator facilities must be imported from Canada. There is no domestic supplier. These pencils are shipped by truck to the irradiation facilities. Although contained in large casks, which provide shielding and protection, they are vulnerable to attack during shipping. A terrorist could use a car or truck bomb and cause an RDD event while in transit. Hijacking the truck is also a possible way to cause serious consequences. These shipments are tracked by law enforcement and radiation control programs, but the security is not as good as for armored trucks that carry cash and other valuables from point to point.

Since armored vehicles have been robbed numerous times, it is reasonable to assume that the trucks carrying these radioactive pencils are at risk. Further, it is not necessary to break into the transport vehicle, only to explode a large bomb next to it.

This scenario would seem to be more probable than attacking an armored car, especially if the attackers were suicidal. (It is reasoned that when the motive for an attack is robbery of money or valuables, a suicide attack can be ruled out.)

In the hypothetical irradiator scenario, the irradiation facility was shut down to rearrange the rods. Since no sterilization work can be accomplished while this is being done, the employees that normally would be working at the site are often furloughed for the duration of the rework. Only the technicians actually performing the rearrangement of the rods and security people are on site. The scenario illustrates how, given a relatively short time to work at the pool, the radioactive pellets can be removed, transferred to a shipping container, and stolen. The explosive placed in the pool and detonated by Manny as he sits on the plane, is to make it more difficult for law enforcement to determine how many pellets are missing and to slow down the investigation, allowing the terrorists to escape and hide the stolen material. Manny would presumably have degrees or education in engineering and possibly physics. Given the large number of foreign students that graduate from U. S. colleges each year, it is highly likely that someone like Manny exists.

Once this material is taken and secreted away, it could be used for a number of terrorist attacks. An RDD might be the most likely use, but there are several other ways the terrorist can utilize this material to cause large consequences, such as hiding it in public places to cause massive exposures to people. Once the material is discovered missing, this alone would cause some public terror. If a large amount of dangerous material were stolen, the public would presumably be told; otherwise, there would be serious consequences, especially with respect to future credibility of government, when this information was found out by the press at a later time. It is difficult to predict how the media would react to stolen material, but since this would be a lead story for many days, the consequences would undoubtedly be severe.

If terrorists succeed in obtaining the material, they could use it at a later time and place of their choosing. Interdiction of terrorist events is difficult once the wherewithal to mount the attack is secured; they have the element of surprise. Further, the terrorists could disrupt our lives by calling in false information regarding planned attacks. If law enforcement and the public were aware that radioactive material is in the hands of terrorists, we would be forced to treat every warning of an attack as if it were a certainty. Further, the terrorists would likely contact the news media with false attack information, knowing that law enforcement officials would have to respond.

The scenario presented in this chapter illustrates how a team of terrorists could acquire a large amount of radioactive material for use in weapons of mass disruption (MDW). From earlier discussions, it is evident that such materials may be obtained, probably with less effort and risk, from other applications which utilize similar materials. However, this scenario is presented to illustrate that radioactive materials, no matter how dangerous, cannot be assumed "self-protecting". Conversely, we must assume that our adversaries are skilled and crafty and if we can handle the materials safely, then so can they. Further, the terrorist that is willing to die for their cause is also willing to be exposed to high levels of radiation.

The obvious question is: "Why don't we just eliminate these materials from our society?"

This question has been considered by some of our most knowledgeable experts. For the time being, ignore the fact that radioactive materials exist all over the world, and even if we eliminate their use in the United States, we would still have to cope with the importation of material.

Several years ago, the United States Congress asked the National Research Council (NRC), the research arm of the National Academies of Science and Engineering (NASE), to review the civilian uses of radionuclide radiation sources and recommend potential replacements for sources that pose a high risk to public health or safety in the event of an accident or attack. A report was issued in 2008[43] that addresses this question. The academy reported, "approximately 5,000 devices containing nearly 55,000 high-activity radiation sources are licensed for use today in the United States. The devices are used for cancer therapy, sterilization of medical devices, irradiation of blood for transplant patients, and of laboratory animals for research, nondestructive testing of structures and industrial equipment, and exploration of geologic formations to find oil and gas deposits." Additionally, "Because the array of applications of these radiation sources is so broad and the applications are essential to securing health, safety, and prosperity, the devices are licensed for use and found in every state in the union."

The primary recommendation of the national academies report was to replace cesium-137 (Cs-137) in the form of cesium chloride as it was determined to be the highest security risk of any of the manufactured and natural radionuclides currently in use and considered by the reviewers. This recommendation was based on its dispensability and its presence in population centers across the country. The committee also recommended that the United States Government provide incentives to facilitate the introduction of alternatives for the high-risk radiation sources. The committee also noted that non-radionuclide replacements

---

[43]   Radiation Source Use and Replacement, National Research Council, National Academies Press, 2008, 500 Fifth Street, N.W., Lockbox 285, Washington, D.C. 20055.

exist for nearly all applications of the radiation sources examined, but they may not all be economically viable or feasible.

In other words, it is cheaper to continue to use the existing radioactive materials than to change to safer alternatives. Further, the study was limited to the consideration of materials that could be used to construct an RDD or "dirty bomb". As is demonstrated in the present study, an RDD is not the only use for radionuclides, nor necessarily the most destructive.

As a result of the Energy Policy Act of 2005 (Public Law 109-58), the Nuclear Regulatory Commission is required to provide a report to the President and U.S. Congress by the Radiation Source and Security Task Force. In their 2010 report[44], the following items were listed as Key Accomplishments.

Since 2006, interagency preparedness has increased. Also, interagency coordination and the interagency group's ability to communicate with the public during an emergency have improved with regard to assessing security programs, making risk-significant radioactive sources more secure, and mitigating consequences thereby reducing the potential risk of use by terrorists. For example, the Task Force devised a plan of action for a comprehensive public education campaign with the goals of increasing public understanding of radiological threats and reducing fears, thereby diminishing the impact of a radiological attack and improving response and recovery in its aftermath. The plan includes a comprehensive compendium of existing educational resources and material that can be used to facilitate a public education campaign.

---

[44]   The 2010 Radiation Source and Security Task Force Report, submitted to the President and U. S. Congress by the chairman of the Nuclear Regulatory Commission, on behalf of the Radiation Source and Security Task Force.

As an outcome of coordination efforts between the interagency, it was agreed to transfer all of the public education outreach initiatives to the Federal Emergency Management Agency (FEMA), the lead for the U.S. Government in public communication on issues related to radiation and other hazards. However, the Task Force will continue to support FEMA's progress on this campaign[45] and will stay apprised of its developments.

In 2007-2009, the Task Force conducted a study to assess the feasibility of phasing out the use of Cs-137 in a highly dispersible form (cesium chloride [CsCl]). Considering the results of the study and other input received, *the Task Force concluded that immediate phase-out would not be feasible because the sources are extensively used in a wide range of applications in medicine, industry, and research with significant health benefits to patients.* However, a gradual, stepwise phase-out could be feasible as alternatives become technologically and economically viable and if disposal pathways are identified

Fortunately, the security of these sources has substantively improved with the implementation of security requirements, such as the increased controls, and voluntary facility and device hardening measures. The study identified a path forward that involves a comprehensive multipart approach for further improving the security of and reducing the risks associated with these sources.

The Task Force deemed that sufficient time is required for the development of replacement technologies for certain applications and for the identification of disposal pathways for disused sources. In the interim, measures such as enhancing the physical security of existing devices provide more effective protection of the CsCl sources currently

---

[45]   The authors are not aware of a plan that has been put forward to date. We
        would be interested in learning more about the details of this work.

in use. For example, the NRC is cooperating with the DOE/ National Nuclear Security Administration (NNSA) to provide, on a voluntary basis, physical protection upgrades to existing CsCl irradiators to complement the security afforded through regulatory requirements.

In 2008-2010, the Task Force evaluated alternative technologies for the seven most common risk-significant radioactive devices. It assessed financial incentives, research needs, and the costs and benefits of potential alternative devices. The analysis found that while alternatives exist for some applications, the viability, relative risk reduction achievable, and stage of development of these alternatives vary greatly. Although alternative forms and radionuclides were assessed, further risk reduction might be achieved through alternative technology research and development that focuses on non-radioactive replacement (e.g., x-ray). X-ray technologies were found to be cost-competitive with radionuclide technologies on an annualized cost basis.

The authors note that improvements in small x-ray devices have led to the replacement of radioactive material devices with x-ray devices, such as lead analyzers and bone densitometers. X-ray devices do not emit radiation when turned off and do not pose a radioactive waste problem. Other such replacements are slowly occurring. X-ray devices pose less of a regulatory burden, requiring only registration rather than licensing. Further, they eliminate the expensive, almost intolerable, radioactive waste disposal problem.

However, technological concerns remain with x-ray devices—specifically, product throughput and downtime of the x-ray devices. The study concluded that successful replacement of the radionuclide technologies with alternatives will require different timetables for each application, will need to be incentivized, and will require a coordinated effort among a wide range of stakeholders. As further discussed, the availability of disposal pathways for radioactive sources should be considered before widespread replacement of radioactive sources with alternative technologies occurs.

As can be seen from these Key Accomplishments (see italicized sections), replacement of radionuclides in the public sector will take many years to accomplish, if ever. Further, everyone appears to agree that financial (or regulatory) incentives will be required to force commercial operators to change. Given the current budget deficit and the legislative climate to reduce both spending anti-business regulation, it is difficult to imagine that either funding or regulation legislation will be enacted in the foreseeable future.

CHAPTER 10 ▨▨▨▨▨▨▨▨▨▨▨▨▨

FIGHTING BACK

To this point, we have painted a very bleak picture of Mass Disruption Weapons. It is not our intention to cause fear and panic, but rather to convince the reader that there is much less to fear than you might suspect. Now that we have explained the dangers of radiation, the relatively accessible sources of material, and the ways that it can be obtained, let us take each of the scenarios described earlier and evaluate the actual risk to individuals that are exposed. Also, we will compare the risk posed by the terrorist events to everyday risks that we have learned to live with. By doing so, we intend to convince you that the risk is much lower than you might expect and when a terrorist event occurs there is no reason to panic or overreact.

In Chapter 2, we presented a scenario in which a terrorist obtains an entry-level job at a hospital and befriends the staff, including the night guards. He learns where radioactive materials are stored and as much about security procedures as possible. He, along with two accomplices, plans, and executes the theft of cobalt-60 material used in a blood irradiator. The three terrorists transport this material into New York City and set off an explosion.

The authors believe that it is likely that a homegrown terrorist or even a foreign-born terrorist could obtain employment in a hospital such as described. It is also likely that such people exist in the United States and are willing to attempt such a mission. However, because of the security currently employed in hospitals that have this amount of radioactive material, it is likely that a terrorist will be detected if they attempted to remove the Co-60 from the blood irradiator. The NRC is sponsoring a program to retrofit these machines with enhanced security devices that make it extremely difficult to remove the radioactive materials and spirit them away. This program is not scheduled to be completed until 2016[46], thereby leaving a number of facilities vulnerable for the interim.

If the terrorists are discovered in the act of stealing the Co-60, it is assumed that they would explode their improvised explosive device in the hospital, causing a fire, and scattering the radioactive materials. The ensuing fire would presumably result in a smoke plume that would spread contamination in the area around the hospital. In this scenario, the terrorist would partially succeed in their mission. The hospital would be severely damaged and the fire would cause major damage. However, unless hospital employees, patients or first responders were close to the explosion, no fatalities would be expected. The nuclear material could be

---

[46] In testimony before the House Committee on Homeland Security, Subcommittee on Emerging Threats, Cybersecurity, and Science and Technology on September 14, 2009, Kenneth Sheely described a program to increase security for blood irradiators (Cesium-137, or Cs-137) and gamma knives (Cobalt-60, or Co-60). One key finding of their work was that radioactive sources within self-shielded cesium irradiators could be extracted more quickly than initially thought. A delay kit (In-Device Delay or IDD) was developed to "make it orders of magnitude more difficult for an adversary to illicitly access and steal the radiological source." As of the time of the hearing, 840 such cesium devices were in use in the United States. At the time of the hearing, only 32 had been hardened under the program. The remaining 808 irradiators "can be hardened by FY2016". It was also stated, "each of these 840 Cs-137 irradiators has enough material that could be used in several RDDs of national significance."

cleaned up in a couple of months and the downwind effects due to the smoke would be minimal.

No off-site radiation exposure would be expected. The area around the hospital would naturally be evacuated and there would be extensive monitoring of the area to insure that all traces of radioactive material were removed. However, this event would be no more severe than if the hospital was hit by a tornado, for example. Further, depending on the location, the probability of the terrorist event occurring at the hospital is much lower than a tornado. The radioactive material can be removed and the area decontaminated. There is no reason to panic.

In this scenario, the terrorists obtain the Co-60 and transport it to New York City. If we postulate that law enforcement officers succeed in identifying the escape vehicle and attempt to interdict the terrorists, we have assumed that the terrorists would drive to a relatively populated area and set off the explosive. This would definitely spread some radioactive material in the area of the explosion, but the consequences would probably be less than if the explosion occurred at the hospital. No major structure fire would be expected and areas near highways tend to have lower population density than hospital neighborhoods.

Now assume that the terrorists are approaching New York City. Radiation detectors are present at most entry points and the truck would probably be identified as carrying radioactive material. Law enforcement would presumably stop the vehicle for further inspection. While the terrorists could explode the truck, the consequences would not be as great as if they exploded it in the hospital. Law enforcement officers would have some control over where they chose to stop the vehicle and thus could force the terrorists to explode the IED in a more remote location. If the terrorists chose to explode the vehicle in the Holland Tunnel, for example, the radioactive material would be confined to a relatively small area and could be cleaned up quickly. The event would result in massive traffic problems for a short time, but there would be no long lasting effects.

Finally, if we assume that the terrorists succeed in getting to the downtown location that they selected to achieve the maximum consequences, the explosion would not be expected to result in large numbers of fatalities or serious injuries. First responders often carry radiation monitors and the site would immediately be cordoned off and evacuated. Clean-up can be effected in a relatively short time and, assuming that the public is convinced that it is safe to return to the area, it would be business as usual in a week or two after the event. In short, while the event would cause significant damage and possible fatalities or serious injuries because of the initial explosion, the consequences would be no worse than many natural disasters.

In Chapter 3, we described an attack using a private plane flown into a downtown office building. If we assume the radioactive material can be obtained (the irradiator scenario of Chapter 9 provides one way that terrorists can obtain relatively large quantities of material), it is difficult if not impossible to stop such an event. There are thousands of private airports in the United States as well as private airfields or landing areas that can be used to launch such an attack. It is not feasible to require radiation monitors at all locations and, in the case of private landing sites, there is no security. We must assume that an event such as this has a finite probability of occurring and it cannot be prevented with one-hundred percent certainty. If you think such an event is not possible, then recall that Joseph Andrew Stack crashed a small plane into an Austin, Texas building containing Internal Revenue Service offices on February 18, 2010. Had Stack included radioactive material, the aftermath would have been greatly exacerbated.

However, the risk is low. The event can be remediated quickly and the affected area can be made safe in days. This is a risk we are going to have to learn to live with. One is much more likely to die by lightning strike or snakebite. (The odds of dying by lightning strike are approximately one in 84,000, snake or other venomous bite, one in 100,000. However, the odds of dying by falling down are reported to be a relatively high one in 246.[47] Our readers are warned to be extremely cautious when falling.) Terrorism risk is lower by factors of thousands. The United States is ranked 33rd in the world by Maplecroft[48], a risk assessment consulting firm in the United Kingdom. Maplecroft has developed a metric they refer to as the Terrorism Risk Index which purports to provide companies with reliable estimates of terrorism risk to human security and international assets. We have already recounted most of the deaths due to terrorism in the United States in this book. The probability of dying from a terrorist event is extremely low.

In Chapter 11, we describe a terrorist event in which radioactive sources are stolen and are placed on the subway or Metro. This event is designed to disrupt normal transit in large metropolitan areas and to reduce ridership. The terrorist also hopes to force authorities to greatly increase security, install radiation monitors in all public transportation systems, and, in general, create a security system such as we now have at airports. This would be the death of public transportation, as we know it. In order to be effective, ground transportation must have quick access and egress. If one has to line up and go through security checks, remove shoes, wait through searches of personal items and, in all likelihood, be prevented from taking many personal items (shoppers carry home groceries, cleaning supplies, etc., etc.), the terrorists have won.

---

[47] The Odds of Dying, Robert Roy Britt, 06 January 2005, Livescience. Figures are for U. S. residents and are compiled from a number of highly reliable sources. http://www.livescience.com/3780-odds-dying.html

[48] Maplecroft, The Towers, St. Stephens Road, Bath, BA1 5JZ, U. K.

Most seasoned travelers have accepted occasionally being exposed to radiation as they prepare to board aircraft, but being exposed several times a day simply to ride local public transportation is clearly unacceptable. Every time we spend an extra hour at airports going through security, it is a harsh reminder that the terrorists have already caused us irreparable damage. If we impose further, possibly Draconian, measures to be instituted if radioactive materials are employed, the terrorists will have used these weapons of mass disruption to successfully disrupt our way of life. Additionally, the cost will be astronomical in terms of the cost of increased security, monitoring equipment and especially, loss of productivity.

It is worthwhile to compare nuclear power plant release events to the postulated terrorist scenarios discussed above. In our postulated terrorist events, we conclude that while the terrorist can cause significant consequences, the number of fatalities and serious injuries will be very low and the affected areas can be remediated quickly. Monetary consequences due to loss of access to the facilities involved, and denial of services, assuming that the public does not overreact, will be relatively small. There will be a short clean-up period and repair of damage to structures caused by the IED, but these consequences will be no more damaging than natural disasters that occur all too frequently.

In short, the real consequences of having a terrorist attack using radioactive materials are quite low. We can recover from an attack quickly and the *physical* residual effects will be minimal. However, if we panic and become paranoid trying to avoid a future attack, we can make our lives miserable and greatly increase the national debt trying to throw money at the problem.

CHAPTER 11

CALCULATING THE RISK

Crawford Smith tugged on the sleeve of his coveralls and finally they slid off his sweaty back. It had been a long one and the Texas heat had just about enervated him. He wiped his face on the driest part of the orange coverall he could find and threw them into the back of the truck. As he pulled on his white tee shirt, he called out across the parking lot, "Hey, Jimmy. Let's get a cold one on the way home."

"Can't do it, Fish. I got to be home early tonight. The ol' lady has plans. You go on and I'll catch you next time."

"You know I can't drive the truck without you. Come on. One quick one can't hurt."

"I got a better idea. You drop me at the 7-11 and I'll call Sue to come by and get me. She's at her mother's and it's on the way. It can't hurt nothing. You're a big boy. You can take the truck back tonight. There ain't nobody there after seven. Just put the sources back in the safe and lock up."

Smith climbed into the cab and started the engine. The air conditioner kicked in on high and they pulled onto the service road and headed for the Houston suburb of Pasadena.

"That paycheck ought to be in the bank by now, Jim ol' boy, and I think I might spend a little of it tonight. Thank Goodness for the computer."

The Friday traffic is bad, as usual, but they finally get to the turn-off.

"Just drop me here, Fish. Hand me the clipboard. I'll sign us out at 9:00. You think you'll be back to the shop by then?"

"Make it 10:00. I know that'll cover me."

Smith pulls into TexiAnn's Dew Drop Inn about six-thirty. The parking lot is almost full, but he finds a spot under a shade tree on the furthermost reaches of the lot. He locks the truck and heads toward a one-story rambling building that has seen better days. The neon beer signs were barely visible in the still bright Texas sunlight.

The smell of stale beer mingled with cigarette smoke, cheap after-shave, and cheaper perfume makes Smith salivate as he pushes open the door. Chilled air rushes past him until the door closes. It takes about half a minute for his eyes to adjust to the dim; he heads toward the bar and looks for standing room. The three bartenders never stop moving, seemingly oblivious to a picket fence of hairy arms waving twenty dollar bills and calling out the names of beer.

Finally, a long neck Shiner Bock is delivered and his change, in the form of wet one-dollar bills, is deposited on the bar to mark his place. The first swig is always the best, and he makes it a long one.

It is almost midnight before Crawford remembers that his pickup is still at the shop and he hasn't taken the truck back. He turns to his new friend and tries to explain why he needs to leave. The words are a little confused, but he finally gets the thought across.

"Why don't I go with you?" We'll pick up your truck and come right back. This joint don't close 'till the sun comes up."

"Why not," says Smith, and they walk out the door together.

Smith pulls into the parking lot at M & M Rad Services and drives around to the back of the building. The rest of the radiography trucks are parked neatly in a line. The only other vehicle in the lot is his Ford F-150 with the mini-camper on the back. After a couple of tries, he backs his truck into the lineup and pops open the door.

"Wait here. I'll unlock the shop and put the sources back. Then we're out of here."

Smith opened the rear doors to the shop and turned on the overhead. *Nobody home. No shocker there, he thought.*

As he turned to head back to the truck, his passenger was standing in the doorway. He looked a second time and finally it dawned on him that the man was holding what looked like a 357 in his right hand. Handcuffs hung from the left.

"Get over by the stove, kid. Move it."

Smith felt the cobwebs clear as adrenalin began to replace the alcohol in his bloodstream. He sidled toward the kitchen area watching his new friend. Neither man seemed nearly as drunk now.

I'm gonna cuff you to the gas pipe. Don't try to break it or you could gas yourself in the process. If you blow the place up, so be it."

"You aint gonna' leave me here are you?"

"You got it, kid. Maybe somebody will decide to come to work tomorrow. Or maybe Sunday. At any rate, you can last 'till Monday. You got enough beer in you so you won't die of thirst. Have a good weekend."

The stranger walked over to the "safe" where the other cameras (as the containers are called in radiography) containing radioactive material were stored. He pulled three stored cameras out and added them to the back of Crawford's truck. He locked the truck and went back to the storage safe and secured it with a heavy duty padlock that he had brought with him. *That should add a few more hours before discovery,* he thought.

Finally, he walked over to Crawford Smith and pointed the gun at his head.

"Where's the GPS transmitter, kid?"

"What do you mean?" responded Smith nervously.

"Cut the crap. Where is the homing device? I know there's one on the truck. Don't make me get rough."

"It's under the hood", said Smith resignedly.

"Thanks, kid. I don't need any unexpected company tonight. I have a lot of ground to cover by morning."

The stranger turned off the lights, closed and locked the door, and returned to the service truck. He slowly crossed the parking lot, stopped, and looked both ways, then nonchalantly headed toward the interstate.

It was later determined that four sources were missing. Crawford Smith is severely disciplined. A similar case occurred in Corpus Christi, Texas, on the same weekend with five sources missing, although it was a different company. Another case occurred in Louisiana. A radiography crew was followed from their offices to a remote work location. They were overwhelmed by two heavily armed men and their radiography truck and two cameras were taken. None of the eleven sources were recovered.

Several weeks later, a call is received at the Washington, D.C. metro headquarters at six o'clock on a Monday morning. The caller states that radioactive material has been hidden on several cars on the metro trains and people will die unless all trains are evacuated immediately. When pressed for more information, the caller tells the operator to look on car # 1020 on the Red Line.

A search of car # 1020 results in finding a single pellet of Iridium-192 material duct taped under a seat. The metro is shut down and all lines are evacuated. Passengers are not told why they are being evacuated. The Washington Post, local television stations, and National Public Radio receive anonymous calls at seven o'clock that morning with a tip that radioactive material has been planted on all cars of the metro. Everyone coming in close proximity to the material will incur severe doses of radiation that can lead to cancer or death. Further, this is a terrorist attack and all public transportation across the United States is targeted.

Over the next month, two other pellets are found on public transportation systems. Both incidents cause major disruption in public transportation. The Department of Homeland Security increases security at entrances to subways and other major public transportation systems. Ridership falls to record low levels. The cost of increased security is estimated to be in the billions of dollars. Traffic problems increase dramatically.

Investigations reveal that the terrorists use Stanley stainless steel thermos bottles with lead shielding to bypass radiation monitors. Since the highly radioactive pellets are mounted on short, steel cables, the terrorists are able to plant the sources without significant exposure to themselves. Merely touching the pellet for a couple of seconds will cause a severe radiation burn around the point of contact. For three of the pellets, sitting in a chair with a planted pellet for 30 minutes or more would cause death, as well as severe radiation burns. Empty containers are found in waste cans in the subway. The terrorists concentrate on cold-weather cities because public transportation is more prevalent and cold-weather clothing can be used to conceal the containers. The media is relentless in reporting the story. Hospital emergency rooms and other medical facilities are swamped with people claiming radiation illness—although few were found to have been exposed. Members of Congress vow to completely eliminate the possibility of future attacks. Foreign press, including Al Jazeera, airs the story worldwide. Several terrorist organizations issue press releases claiming responsibility. The terrorists are never apprehended.

*   *   *

We can greatly reduce the risk posed by the use of radioactive materials by terrorists and we should begin immediately. This does not have to be a costly and time-consuming process, but it requires the cooperation of all of us including the public, licensees of MIAN materials, first responders, law enforcement, public officials, and especially the media.

Before we discuss how to reduce risk, we need to understand how one defines risk. Most of us consider risk as a relatively simple concept. If we are sitting at home in our easy chair watching TV or reading a book, we are "safe". We do not expect anything untoward to happen to us. Familiar things surround us and our home is secure. We are not "at risk". However, if we expand our horizons slightly, we might consider more than safety and security from accident or attack from unknown assailants. Are we at risk from some other events or possible consequences? Have we been exposed to disease or an infectious virus? Is someone planning to file a lawsuit that could cost hundreds or thousands of dollars to settle? Are we a candidate for a heart attack or stroke? We could be at risk from these or a multitude of other maladies or malevolent, malicious, or malignant events.

The risk management expert defines risk as a combination of three ingredients or numbers. These include:

1) The probability that the event will happen
2) The probability that the event will succeed in causing bad consequences.
3) The magnitude or extent of the consequences

When your insurance company sells you fire insurance or automobile insurance, they have done their research and they know your risk level. Your insurance cost is based on the risk they calculate. For example, the insurance company has calculated the probability of having a fire in your city or town and probably in your zip code and maybe in your tract. They know how many fires happen in your area every year and they estimate the likelihood that your home will catch fire. That number is the probability that the fire will happen, item 1 above. Let's assume it is one in one thousand or 1/1000.

Next, they know how much your home is worth. This is the actual value of the house, excluding the land. This should include the replacement cost of the dwelling. It may include the contents and living expenses while you are waiting to move back into the house. This number is item 3, the maximum expected consequences. For the purpose of this example, assume the structure and contents is worth $100,000, just to make the math simple.

The last number is the probability that the maximum consequences will actually happen, given that a fire happens. This number includes such things as whether your house has a sprinkler system, how far you are from the fire station, or if there is a fire department or volunteers, etc. These elements are used to determine the expected extent of damage. For example, if you live next door to the fire house and you have an automatic sprinkler system installed, the insurance company might assume that you will lose only 50% of your total home value in a fire. If you live out in the country and there is no fire department, the insurance company might assume that the house will be a complete loss if it catches fire. Let's assume, in this example, that the odds indicate that we will lose only 50% of the house value if we have a fire; the fire department will put out the fire before it consumes the entire structure and contents.

Now, we can calculate the risk. The risk, on a yearly basis, which will be assumed by the insurance company if we purchase their insurance coverage, is:

Risk = (Prob. of occurrence) x (percentage loss) x (Cost or replacement)

$$= (1/1000) \times (.50) \times (100,000) = \$50.00$$

The insurance company thus (over)charges us $500 per year for insurance; they keep the rest for commissions, overhead, and legal fees for their attorneys when they refuse to pay and we sue them. (This is an exaggeration, of course. They really charge much more. That is why insurance companies are normally very profitable.) If the above calculations are correct, the insurance company will make money if they insure enough houses and the averaging of all events is correct.

This simple example demonstrates how risks are calculated. Insurance companies use more complex techniques and they have actuaries on the payroll that determine the probability of events happening. They know how long you will live (on average) before they sell you life insurance. They know how often folks get sick and how much it costs to treat them before they set rates for medical insurance. They continually update their predictions from claims. Thus, insurance companies become experts at calculating risk because managing risk is their business.

The point of this discussion is to illustrate how risk is calculated. Once we define risk using a mathematical formula, we can analyze the components of risk and perform something called risk management. In the final analysis, our goal is to manage terrorist risk. We know we cannot eliminate it completely. We are aware that we cannot spend a trillion dollars a year on terrorist risk or we lose. The terrorist will have beaten us without even firing a shot. Thus, we must learn to *manage risk. This means we strive to reduce risk to the lowest practical level in the most economical way.* We have to strike a balance between how much risk we are willing to accept and the cost reducing it even further.

An interesting example of risk perception can be demonstrated using the following simple "mind experiment". Most of us have walked atop concrete or brick walls, balancing on the narrow top ledge. If we lose our balance, we jump to the ground, climb back on, and walk along the wall again. Now, assume you are on an identical wall except it is ten stories high. We look down as we take the first step out from safety; our heart begins to beat frantically. We experience an adrenalin rush and suddenly we are no longer relaxed and confident, but we are virtually paralyzed by the fear of falling. We know intellectually that we can walk that wall, as we have done many times before when it was only four feet from the ground. What has changed? We have the same physical ability, thus the probability of success should be the same.

The only part of the risk equation that has changed is the consequences. If we fall from four feet, we are not injured. If we fall from ten stories, we probably die. Thus, keeping everything else constant, the risk increases greatly just by elevating the height of the wall.

As we attempt to reduce terrorist risk, we must consider all of the contributing factors in the risk equation. First, we should reduce the opportunity for a terrorist event to occur. We keep a keen eye out for suspicious behavior. We notice unusual events and report them to law enforcement. We attempt to prevent smuggling, and use common sense to protect MIAN materials. We increase security in all possible areas.

Secondly, we prepare for such an event so that we can mitigate the consequences while the event is happening. We train our first responders to deal with radioactive materials without becoming exposed to unacceptable doses. These actions will decrease the effectiveness of such an event. They will reduce the probability of achieving the worst-case scenario.

Finally, we must reduce the consequences of the event. This includes not only reducing injuries and possible fatalities when the event happens, but also we need to reduce the psychological consequences. We cannot allow the terrorists to deny us access to public places and transportation. We have to go back to the shopping centers and office buildings and resume our normal lifestyle as soon as the authorities deem them safe. Those in positions of authority must remain calm and provide direction. The news media should become part of the solution and not the problem.

In short, the public can mitigate the consequences of a terrorist event by understanding the danger and not overreacting. By reducing the consequences, we reduce the risk and thereby make the event less attractive to the terrorist. We can actually reduce both the risk and the likelihood of the event by not allowing the terrorist to cause panic and terror.

In the next chapters, we will provide additional details and suggestions regarding how to mitigate consequences when a weapon of mass disruption is deployed.

CHAPTER 12

REDUCING THE RISK

Reducing the risk of weapons of mass disruption consists of several steps. First, we need to prevent the terrorist from acquiring MIAN materials. Since there are thousands of sources in the United States alone, the probability of maintaining 100% security is impossible. There will be sites that do not maintain adequate security. Some owners will go bankrupt and leave materials in storage, poorly guarded. Insiders or disgruntled employees will be willing to sell materials to terrorists if offered enough money. Jihadists can find employment at MIAN sites and homegrown terrorists have proven to become terrorists. When a terrorist is willing to die for a cause, it is impossible to prevent them from being successful in obtaining these weapons of mass disruption.

Even if we could protect everything that we know about today, there are lost and misplaced materials that could be used.[49] A search of a radiation control program's records under a state's open records laws would probably reveal a number of "unattended" radiation sources that could potentially be stolen

---

[49]   It was reported on May 2, 2011, that radioactive materials were found by workers at a laboratory at UCLA. The material had apparently been stored "for decades" in a floor vault on the campus. It apparently had been used in a chemistry class. The construction worker was contaminated when he opened the container. No one was aware this material existed.

rather easily. Even in the event we could protect everything in the United States, there is a high probability that a terrorist can smuggle material across the borders. Thus, we must assume that the terrorists will eventually, if they do not already, have possession of MIAN materials. However, this does not mean we should give up and quit trying to keep these materials out of their hands. The more difficult we can make it to get the materials, the better chance we have of discovering they are missing or catching them in the act of obtaining them. Further, terrorists will attempt to optimize their opportunities. If we can make it more difficult to obtain and use MIAN materials, they will turn to another form of terrorism.

Preventing Unauthorized Possession

How do we prevent the use of radioactive material for nefarious purposes? We begin by preventing possession of radioactive material without proper authorization. Most possession and use is through a permit called a "radioactive material license" or a "nuclear materials license", as the US NRC refers to them.

Actually, there are four ways to legally possess radioactive material. Most material is possessed by acquiring a specific radioactive material license from the government regulating body with jurisdiction. Otherwise, the radioactive material must be possessed under a general license, be distributed as an exempt quantity or source, or not be licensable at all.

To acquire a radioactive material license, an application must be submitted to the agency with jurisdiction (US NRC or Agreement State) one must demonstrate technical and financial capability and responsibility during the licensing process. After 9/11, applicants are reviewed to assure that the radioactive material is not going to be used in a frivolous manner. Once the license is issued, the licensee can acquire the specific radioactive material which they are licensed to own (suppliers will not supply it until they confirm there is a valid license issued). The owner of the material can expect to be inspected every one to five years depending on the type of material and how it is used.

Some specific licensees are manufacturers who have an authorization to distribute devices containing radioactive material for use under a "general license". The general license is contained within the rules and regulations of the agency with jurisdiction (which are almost exactly the same for the NRC and each AS). The person or company acquiring a generally licensed device must register its acquisition and use with the applicable agency. They must follow the specific rules and regulations issued for that use. They, too, can expect an inspection, but less frequently than as for a specific license. Generally licensed devices can contain rather large quantities of radioactive material; say as much as five curies. Recently there has been a regulatory effort to minimize this method of controlling the use of radioactive material as it has long been seen as a rather risky method of regulation.

Small quantities of radioactive material are distributed by companies that have specific licenses authorizing the manufacture and distribution of "exempt quantities". Typically, these rather innocuous sources can be handled with a bare hand. They are used for simple applications like supplying a small radiation field to check a radiation survey instrument (such as a Geiger counter) operation, or supplying positively charged alpha particles to remove negative ions from film, smoke detectors, etc. Once distributed, these devices and quantities are no longer regulated, but it would be very difficult to use a collection of them to create a "dirty bomb". We can probably ignore such sources as a possible terrorist weapon.

The fourth manner of possession of radioactive material is from naturally occurring materials found on the Earth's surface. They are also included under the regulated concentrations if the amount of radioactive material is over a certain level. It is not practical to require a person who happens to possess a granite rock (Granite contains elevated levels of the isotope radium-226) to hold a license. Fortunately, most naturally occurring isotopes are of such low concentration that they can be completely ignored. While it is possible to chemically or mechanically concentrate these materials, a great deal of effort and time is required. It is much easier and faster to steal the material needed.

Prior to the terror attacks of September 11, 2001, security of radioactive materials was barely functional. For example, a user of a large industrial source might only be required to have a padlock on the storage container and a written procedure that stated "the material could only be handled by authorized person(s)." Radiation protection was the major concern of radiation regulatory organizations. After 9/11, the security requirements were greatly increased and solidified. For example in July 2002, the DOE/NRC Interagency Working Group on Radiological Dispersal Devices was formed in order to evaluate methods for improving the control of nuclear materials in the United States that could be used for such potential weapons. This led to the publication in May 2003 of the Working Group's first product, "Radiological Dispersal Devices: An Initial Study to Identify Materials of Greatest Concern and Approaches to Their Tracking, Tagging, and Disposition."[50] This study identified the "radioactive materials of greatest concern" and recommended a National Source Tracking System (NSTS), which was later codified into law. Shortly thereafter, in July 2003, the International Atomic Energy Agency (IAEA) issued IAEA-TECDOC-1344, "Categorization of Radioactive Sources", which formalized the

---

[50]   http://www.energy.gov/media/RDDRPTF14MAYa.pdf

Category 1 and Category 2 list of isotopes and quantities that were later adopted in the United States.

The next major step in the United States was the enactment of the Energy Policy Act of 2005.[51] This legislation led to four important developments: (1) the formal requirement for a mandatory radiation source tracking system (NSTS); (2) the issuance of "increased controls" on some licensees possessing certain quantities of Category 1 and Category 2 materials; (3) a requirement for an annual report to the Congress on the increased security, including efforts with the AS; and (4) a requirement for a study by the National Research Council to identify the legitimate uses of high-risk radiation sources and the feasibility of replacing them with lower-risk sources.

Later in 2005, the NRC issued an order requiring the development and implementation of "increased controls" by licensees (both NRC and AS licensees) possessing certain types and quantities of radioactive material. The requirements included more stringent procedures for allowing access to radioactive materials (such as documented background checks of authorized users) and implementation of security systems capable of initiating a timely armed response from a local law enforcement agency.

In 2008, the National Research Council completed its study, "Radiation Source Use and Replacement[52]," which reviewed the current status of the 55,000 or so high-activity sources licensed for use in the United States, concentrating on the four natural or manufactured radionuclides—americium-241, cesium-137, cobalt-60, and iridium-192—that comprise 99% of those sources. While public policy has not followed the recommendations from

---

[51] Public Law 109-58, August 8, 2005
[52] Radiation Source Use and Replacement, National Research Council, National Academies Press, 2008, 500 Fifth Street, N.W., Lockbox 285, Washington, D.C. 20055

that study (the primary recommendation appears to be aggressive replacement of cesium chloride sources), the 2008 National Research Council report contains a wealth of relevant background information.

More recently in 2009, attempts were made to extend the formal NSTS tracking system to Category 3 sources, or to at least some Category 3 sources. However, with a 2-2 deadlock within the NRC, that attempt was blocked. Prior to that, in 2008, fingerprinting and an FBI background check were added to the requirements for licensees subject to increased controls. In recent months, the NRC has become much more active in implementing additional security and control requirements, with a rulemaking in June 2010 to impose physical protection requirements for Category 1 and Category 2 quantities of radioactive material through Title 10 Part 37, of the Code of Federal Regulations (10 CFR 37). This proposed rulemaking is subject to public comment until November 12, 2010, so it does not yet have the force of law. Meanwhile, licensees remain subject to the NRC increased controls orders.

The NRC staff has already produced guidance for licensees on how to meet these proposed new requirements. In particular, Subpart B of the rulemaking addresses background checks, fingerprinting, access authorization, and related requirements. Subpart C is concerned with physical protection during use, and has a requirement for a security program that generally follows the guidance provided in IAEA Nuclear Security Series No. 11[53], "Security of Radioactive Sources, Appendices I (Description of Security Measures) and Appendix II (Examples of Content for

---

53   Developing Safety Culture in Nuclear Activities—Practical Suggestions to Assist Progress Safety Reports Series No. 11, IAEA, Vienna, 1998 http://www.pub.iaea.org/MTCD/publications/PDF/P064_scr.pdf

a Security Plan). Subpart D addresses physical protection in transit. This is a very comprehensive rulemaking that appears to be trying to eliminate some of the existing gaps in the protection of the public health and safety. It is worth noting that, while the proposed 10 CFR 37 rulemaking covers "security program review", no particular requirement for individual licensee risk assessment is included, even though IAEA Nuclear Security Series No. 11 contains an Appendix III (Description of a Vulnerability Assessment).

The NRC imposed additional regulations on the industry in 2005. This program, normally referred to as Increased Controls, identified what is termed "dangerous" levels of various materials. The so-called "D" (D for dangerous) values are based on IAEA defined quantities, except the NRC threshold levels are approximately ten times greater than the levels defined as dangerous by the IAEA. This program requires the licensee to have much greater security and record keeping than for amounts of material that fall below the threshold or cut-off levels. While this is a step in the right direction, it is still possible to obtain "dangerous" levels of materials by stockpiling material from several sources. Further, the guidelines for security are not well defined and the licensees are not normally experts in security. Thus, the regulations may not be fully or correctly implemented, the licensees may be capable of creating a secure facility, and the regulators do not perform site visits often enough to insure that they are actually secure.

A significant effort is currently underway to increase the security of certain, large quantity radioactive materials used in MIAN applications. The Nuclear Regulatory Commission (NRC) has drafted new regulations, contained in 10 CFR 37, for securing such radioactive materials. They are currently receiving comments from the user community and other affected parties, such as state regulators. Based on the comments received to date, it appears that the MIAN community is resisting the proposed new regulations. Even if the proposed changes in regulation are adopted and imposed on users, implementation of the regulations will take time and will add unnecessary overhead and thus cost to the industry.

The National Nuclear Security Administration (NNSA) is also working to improve the security of high-risk radioactive sources. In testimony before the House Committee on Homeland Security, Subcommittee on Emerging Threats, Cybersecurity, and Science and Technology on September 14, 2009, Kenneth Sheely[54] described a program to increase security for blood irradiators (Cs-137) and gamma knives (Co-60). One key finding of their work was that radioactive sources within self-shielded cesium irradiators could be extracted more quickly than initially thought. A delay kit (In-Device Delay or IDD) was developed to "make it orders of magnitude more difficult for an adversary to illicitly access and steal the radiological source." As of the time the hearing, 840 such cesium devices were in use in the United States, but only 32 had been hardened under the program. The remaining 808 irradiators "can be hardened by FY2016". It was also stated, "Each of these 840 Cs-137 irradiators has enough material that could be used in several RDDs of national significance."

In addition to the above programs, the authors have proposed a voluntary program to supplement the increased controls initiative. This program, which is contained in a interactive computer program, includes a screening tool that will aid the licensee in determining if the material is considered dangerous and rank it according to the amount of material and the type of

---

[54]   Kenneth Sheely, Testimony before the House Committee on Homeland Security, Subcommittee on Emerging Threats, Cybersecurity, and Science and Technology on September 14, 2009.

material. This process also considers amounts below the threshold of the NRC increased controls program, assuming that the terrorist could still use the smaller amounts for some attacks, as well as combine amounts from several thefts. The self-assessment tool will also provide metrics so that the licensee can compare the level of security against a standard of safety. The required security level will increase as the amount of material and type of material increases to higher D values. The highlights of this proposed program are presented in Appendix 4.

This program has recently been funded by the Alfred P. Sloan Foundation. The self-assessment tool should be ready in approximately in late 2012. Experience of the authors indicates that voluntary programs are preferred over regulations. Further, regulations set minimum standards for security and rely on inspections to guarantee compliance. Voluntary programs are less invasive and can result in better overall performance. When the responsibility for security is placed on the site, there is a greater likelihood that the person in charge will be more alert to possible ways to steal MIAN materials, screen employees, and look for weaknesses in their system.

When there is a regulatory requirement, the person responsible is more likely to meet the minimum acceptable requirement. Further, it is difficult to justify to superiors spending more than the minimum necessary to meet regulations. If the site control officer is responsible for preventing loss rather than meeting a standard, most people will raise the bar and provide the best practicable security measures. The authors (especially Haygood) have visited numerous sites and interviewed scores of licenses. It is our opinion that most, if not all, of these people want to operate safely and take their jobs very seriously. However, it is also our opinion that they do not want, or require, additional regulation.

CHAPTER 13

WINNING THE WAR ON TERRORISM

If we hope to beat the terrorist at his own game, there are a number of things that can be done. These rules of engagement will not cost much and they will not require much of your time but all of us must participate. This chapter contains some of the things we can do to reduce risk and make the United States a safer place. Law enforcement and Homeland Security are working diligently to identify possible terrorists and stop them before they can obtain MIAN materials. They are our first line of defense and they are very good at what they do. We need to support them in every way and cooperate with programs and regulations.

However, it is impossible to know every potential terrorist, to stop every theft, to interdict every plot and to stop our enemies from smuggling materials across our borders. If we increase the number of law enforcement and homeland security personnel, we increase our costs. Considering that there are probably more than 25,000 sites to protect, many sites have multiple sources, more than one type of material, and some of the material is used by personnel in the field and thus are not always in a secured facility, it is clear that we cannot protect everything using law enforcement alone. Add to this the potential for smuggling materials into the country across borders that extend for thousands of miles, much of which is not under continuous surveillance.

We also must consider the insider who has access to MIAN materials. Background checks will prevent many potential terrorists from having access to MIAN materials, but not everyone. Malik Hasan, the army psychiatrist who killed thirteen people at Fort Hood Texas in 2009 was an Army psychiatrist. He had undergone security background checks. Every psychiatrist goes through a battery of psychological tests and is evaluated by a practicing psychiatrist. While there is evidence that Hasan displayed anti-American traits, the fact remains that all evaluators approved him and allowed him to practice his profession.

We cannot always identify potentially dangerous insiders. The shooting massacres at Columbine High School (April 20, 1999 / 32 killed) and Virginia Tech (April 16, 2007 / 33 killed) provide examples of individuals that posed grave anger but were not stopped in time to avoid bloodshed. The fact is, we cannot expect to stop every attempt by terrorists to obtain and use MIAN materials. When asked about his country's defenses against attack, Napoleon is reputed to have stated, "If I protect everything, I protect nothing." If we spread ourselves so thin attempting to protect everything, we will not succeed. Further, if we spend billions of dollars to attempt to defend everything, the threat of terrorism has already succeeded in costing us part of our fortune and some of our freedom. This brings us to the most important question of all.

What can we do to reduce the risk?

Politicians and public employees

We need leadership, not rhetoric. Use common sense and address the problem head-on. Statements like "we will never allow this to happen again" or "we will do whatever it takes to protect our citizens" do not solve anything. We cannot reduce the risk to absolute zero. There is always risk in everything we do. Spending us into poverty is not the answer to all problems. We, the constituents, are ultimately responsible for preventing terrorist events. Of course, we need to regulate and provide support for law enforcement and first responders, etc. However, there is no substitute for citizen vigilance. What we need is levelheaded, common sense response. Provide reliable and timely information regarding the ongoing clean-up and how we can get back to normal as soon as possible. We are a resilient people and we respond to adversity well. Leadership in time of adversity is key. Making un-kept promises is not.

The role of law enforcement

Another tactic that could help prevent the misuse of radioactive material is to improve coordination and communication with local government entities, such as city and county administrations, and police, sheriff, and fire departments.

Radiation control agencies generally have a good handle on the movement and use of radioactive material, as well as the potential threats of their misuse or targeting. However, local police and municipal authorities typically have no greater knowledge of the surrounding circumstances than the general populace. Reported theft or loss of radioactive material usually results only in the filing of a report. The potential consequences of such a loss of control of material does not seem to register with the local authorities very well. The only attempt at coordination with local government is when the regulatory agencies advise licensees to contact the local fire departments and coordinate emergency response issues with them. After all, it would not be a good circumstance for emergency personnel to not respond to a heart attack victim in a facility simply because there are "Caution—Radiation" signs posted at the entrance. Nor would firefighters want to attempt to extinguish a fire when there is a possibility that radioactive material might be involved.

States have emergency response systems set up for response to tornados, hurricanes, earthquakes, etc. The US NRC requires nuclear power plants to work with their states and incorporate/integrate their emergency response plans into those of the state. This usually includes radiation emergency training for state and local authorities and personnel. Periodic drills and exercises are conducted to maintain competence of all of the teams. If this same approach could be taken (although on a more limited basis) to have licensees work with local authorities and set up emergency response plans and provide some training, an effective response to terrorist actions would be better assured. Perhaps video training packages would be helpful in this process.

As a minimum, good channels of communication should be set up between the licensees and the various authorities that they may need to deal with. For any chance to deal with terrorists' actions successfully, local authorities, law enforcement, and emergency response personnel need prompt reporting and they need to be kept informed by persons knowledgeable in radiation matters.

Transportation of MIAN materials

Radioactive material stolen to be transported to another area and used as a weapon could only be transported by air or ground vehicle. For air, a helicopter would be the most useful vehicle. This would probably not be very likely, but it would be possible. If this method were used, we would be unlikely to discover the transport. However, the appearance of a helicopter at a scene where radioactive material was stolen would be quite conspicuous as there are not very many helicopters flying around. Transport of stolen material by car or truck is far more likely, and perhaps more convenient to the terrorist. This would mean that monitoring highways and roadways would allow a method of discovering such transport. We cannot monitor every roadway in the country; it would be cost prohibitive. We can, however, set up radiation monitoring stations at key locations in our highway systems and increase our chances of detecting illegal transport. In fact, this is already done to some extent. We can also periodically fly aircraft with sensitive detectors over major highways to look for such transport. And this is also already being done to some extent.

There are several problems associated with remote and aerial radiation monitoring. One is that there are many legal shipments of radioactive material on our highways that might generate "false positives". Authorities would waste a great deal of time responding to legitimate transport. Second, is that this is an expensive process. Flying of aircraft is not cheap and instruments capable of detecting radiation at rather great distances are expensive and delicate. These steps, however, would probably be good for known theft and suspected transport.

Licensees

The licensees who use radioactive materials are clearly the first line of defense. Radiation safety officers must take their jobs seriously and meet the intent, not just the letter of regulations. The authors believe that most licensees are dedicated to protecting the materials in their possession. The current increased controls requirements promulgated by the Nuclear Regulatory Commission covers "dangerous quantities" of radioactive materials. However, smaller amounts, added together can prove just as great a danger and, since the requirements for security are lower, the material would be easier to obtain. The authors have developed a security assessment tool that can be used by the licensee to evaluate the effectiveness of their security system. This tool will also indicate areas that should be strengthened. This voluntary approach places the responsibility for security on the licensee and not on the regulator. The licensee may not have a dedicated security staff. This tool is designed to be used by non-security personnel.

Finally, the second most important thing a licensee can do, just behind great security, is to report the loss of materials as soon as possible. We are most vulnerable when the terrorist has materials that they can use against us and no one knows it. The licensees should immediately report missing materials. This implies that they should check for missing material often. Do not allow materials to become orphans. Dispose of material no longer needed. Remember, you are the first line of defense.

The Media

The media will be very important when a terrorist event occurs. We get our news almost instantaneously today. Our smart phones have email and web browsers. In the event of a terrorist attack that involves radioactive materials, there will be a news blitz. This is good because it will prevent people from approaching the affected area. The media must show restraint. This is not a political event. It is not about Republicans or Democrats. It is an attack on our way of life and we have to fight back to prevent the terrorists from winning. The media should not suggest that the authorities are holding back information or downplaying the seriousness of the event, nor should they publish "information" based on supposition.

When the Fukushima event was in the news every day, all day, a common theme was that the public was not being told, " . . . how bad the situation actually is . . ." The news media constantly used terms like "we don't really know how bad the radiation levels are", and "if you can believe the power company", etc. This type of reporting undermines the confidence of the public and causes more fear and terror. It is journalism at its worst. This kind of reporting sensationalizes the event and is done for only one reason-to sell advertising. If the media exacerbates the event, they are pawns of the terrorist. We have a right to know the unvarnished truth. We do not want it hyped or minimized.

No matter how bad the event, we are always better off knowing the extent of the problem. We can and do imagine far worst. If you call in an expert to discuss the event, use one that is qualified and does not use hyperbole. We deserve someone who is rational, reasoned, calm, and truthful. When you use our public airways, which are owned by us all, you owe us a commitment to truth.

The Public

Everyone must be vigilant and be aware of the potential for an attack using MIAN materials. Notice when someone is acting in an unusual manner. If you work around radioactive materials, treat them as if they were a weapon and prevent them from falling into the hands of those who will do us harm. If you suspect someone, tell the authorities. It is far better to be overly cautious than to ignore signs that could be symptomatic of terrorist preparation. After the 9/11 events, there were a number of people who recalled things that were unusual; reporting them could have resulted in preventing the attack. For example, one terrorist who was taking flying lessons indicated he was not interested in take-off or landing, just being able to steer the plane.

Obviously, this remark, taken alone, would not constitute a red flag warning. However, combined with other information such as the nationality of the individual, his attitude, and conversations that normally occur during extended face to face meetings, a perceptive person could suspect that the student may be planning an attack.

If in doubt, report it.

You

Prepare yourself and your family. Set up a family plan to deal with emergencies. Maintain a supply of emergency supplies and materials to deal with emergencies that might occur in your area—including a radiological attack. Establish a location for your family to assemble. Determine how best to acquire assistance from authorities (radio, TV, etc.) and train your family to cooperate with the authorities. Educate yourself and your family members so that none of you will panic and put yourselves in more dangerous or threatening conditions.

Everyone

Use common sense. In our interviews with licensees that use radioactive materials in their business, possibly the most memorable was with a woman who was president of an industrial radiography company. She complies with the regulations for handling and storing MIAN materials and is under increased controls. However, she is not satisfied with just meeting the minimum requirements. She comes in to her office early on random days and observes her employees as they handle the materials. These random checks are not required by the regulatory agency, but they keep the employees from becoming complacent.

An anecdote she related to us during our interview made a great impression on the authors. During the ice storms that hit Texas in the winter of 2010-2011, she refused to let the trucks go out to work sites. She reasoned that these trucks could become mired in traffic if the roads were closed and possibly abandoned by her employees in the event of severe cold. When she received a call from a disgruntled client, she told him why she had decided not to send out her crews. Instead of being angry, the client understood and complimented her for her foresight. She had risked losing a client because she was not willing to risk having the radioactive material stolen. This behavior cannot be forced by regulation; it is a result of using common sense and being proactive to protect potentially dangerous materials.

Trust the authorities. When a terrorist event happens, we must be willing to accept the information provided by competent members of the government and regulators. If we assume that we are not being told information about the level of risk, we are being terrorized. If we overreact and make a bad situation worse, we have succumbed to the terrorist.

When a terrorist event occurs, you have just been drafted into the war on terror. We will be fighting them on our soil. We must follow the lead of those in charge. If we don't trust them, now is the time to make it known, not after the event happens. When we are told we can return to the site of the event, have the courage to return to normal and put the event behind you. Accept the risk and move on. If we do not, we lose. It will take courage to shake off the memory of the attack and go back to work, shop, or frequent the affected area.

If we allow the terrorist to change our lifestyle, cause us to spend large amounts of money or keep us from enjoying our freedom to move about, we lose.

CHAPTER 14

SUMMARY

The purpose of this book is to make as many people as possible aware of the danger of using radioactive materials for weapons of mass disruption. Our innate fear of the unknown, especially all things radioactive, makes these materials the perfect weapon of choice for terrorist organizations. With the elimination of Osama bin Laden there is hope that Al Qaeda will gradually fade away. However, previous experience in the Middle East indicates that change is difficult to affect and hard to predict.

The Palestinian/Israeli conflict shows no sign of permanent solution. The recent Arab Spring uprisings in the Middle East give us reason to hope that these countries are ready to throw off their traditional dictatorial and theocracy based governments and adopt a western style of democracy. However, it remains to be seen what will emerge from the chaos that currently exists.

Democracy means choice and sometimes we may not agree with the choices that are made. The Muslim Brotherhood (MB), the largest political opposition organization in many Arab states, has as its slogan "Islam is the Solution". Founded in 1928, their goal is to instill the Qur'an as the sole reference point for ordering the life of the Muslim family, including individual, community and state. The MB requires all members to allocate a portion of their income to the movement. Many members live in oil-rich countries, a powerful source of revenue. If this organization were to gain a foothold in a number of Arabic countries, it could result in a coalition of Arabic nations governed by Muslim theocracy, posing an even greater threat than we currently have.

Even if Al Qaeda as an organization is mortally wounded, which has not yet been proven, the threat of splinter organizations and small cells operating autonomously still exists. In fact, if these groups are cut off from the main organization, they become harder to detect and more difficult to predict. The determination to avenge the death of Osama bin Laden can be a great incentive. There are many followers that would consider it a great honor to give their lives to punish the United States for killing their founder and leader.

The struggle to assert one's beliefs over another's is not new. Christians and Moslems have been at odds for at least 1,000 years. There are many who think the basic mistrust between these, the two largest religions in the world, continues to grow. There is a basic and profound difference in belief between these religions that cannot be resolved by mutual agreement. As long as both sides consider the other irreconcilably incorrect in their beliefs, and their beliefs are extremely important to them, there can be no true harmony. There are strong adherents for both religions, who can be termed as fundamentalists. The strong believers will on both sides show no signs of resolving the differences in belief and appear to be more than willing to engage in armed conflict rather than peaceful and rational compromise.

The concept of Jeffersonian democracy is not likely to be adopted, in the view of the writers, in Arabic countries in the near future, if ever. One of the authors (Jones) has traveled rather extensively in Arabic countries and has personally discussed these points with many acquaintances from these countries. In Moslem countries, there is a strong reliance on traditional tribal customs that is often not appreciated by Westerners. The concept of the tribe as a cohesive unit, headed by a Sheik or the equivalent, is ingrained in their society. The tribe is an extension of the family and loyalty is expected and rewarded. This is one reason why we have a difficult time infiltrating the ranks of the military. Trust is reserved for members of the extended family. Outsiders need not apply.

And, lest we forget them, there are other terrorists of which we must be wary. There are eco-terrorists, the haters of Jews, gays, politicians, strong government, law enforcement, and any type of authority. There are those who hope society will disintegrate and we will revert to survival of the prepared, namely, them. There are criminals and psychopaths that are looking for enrichment or notoriety. We do not have a shortage of potential enemies.

However, we will persevere. The most important thing to remember if you read this book is that we must have the courage to continue with our way of life in spite of terrorism. When we have an attack that involves radioactive materials, do not panic. Do not overreact, and do not let it change your lifestyle. Fight back by staying the course. Courage is a word that many famous people have tried to define.

Some notable attempts include:

Courage is the price that Life exacts for granting peace.
Amelia Earhart, Courage, 1927

Courage is doing what you're afraid to do. There can be no courage unless you're scared.
Eddie Rickenbacker (1890-1973)

Courage is resistance to fear, mastery of fear-not absence of fear.
Mark Twain (1835-1910)

And to the media,

Keep your fears to yourself, but share your courage with others.
                                        Robert Lewis Stevenson (1850-1894)

And finally, for all of us,

But screw up your courage to the sticking place.
                                        Shakespeare, Macbeth (act 1, scene 7)

When a terrorist event happens, don't get scared, get mad.

AFTERWORD ▪▪▪▪▪▪▪▪▪▪▪▪

EXPERIENCES, THOUGHTS,
AND CONCERNS OF THE AUTHORS

JAMES WILLIAM JONES

James William Jones earned a Ph.D. in mechanical engineering, founded several successful companies, and served as a white House Fellow with the Office of Science and Technology Policy. He and his wife live in Huntington Beach, California. This is his third book.

The following comments are provided by Jones based upon his experience working and traveling in several countries in the Middle East. The opinions expressed herein are purely his own.

The "conversations" are a compilation of various anecdotes that I remember from my travels. There were many, similar conversations, but these are the ones I can recall.

As an instructor in engineering technology used in the oil industry, I have traveled to the Middle East quite a number of times starting in the late 1980's. My training classes are approximately one week long and I spend a day or two at the beginning and end of the course recovering from jet lag or waiting for the next available flight. I was in Kuwait before their invasion by Iraq and afterward. The change in the Kuwaitis was remarkable. The people were much subdued by the invasion. They lost much of their braggadocio and the beginning of humility was evident if you looked close enough. Before the war, they told me they were rich enough to buy off both the Iraqis and Iran; they were contributing to both. They soon found that did not work as well as they planned.

My first inkling of Osama bin Laden was in 1998. I was teaching a short course at a hotel in Kuwait City. When I returned from a class, there was a letter slipped under the door of my hotel room. It was from the American Embassy informing me that some chap named bin Laden was looking to kidnap Americans. I had no idea who this gentleman was and did not learn until September 11, 2001.

In addition to Kuwait, I have visited Saudi Arabia, Dubai, Abu Dhabi, and most of the rest of the United Arab Emirates (UAE). I have traveled to Egypt a number of times, including taking my family on vacation to Cairo. I make a point of getting to know my students, and I spend evenings and weekends talking to the locals and seeing the sights. My students are typically very hospitable and I have enjoyed many dinners with a table of students discussing politics, our culture, their culture, and occasionally engineering. Most of my students have traveled extensively in the United States. They know our culture as well as a foreigner can. I have been proselytized concerning becoming a Muslim and have been given several books written especially for the purpose. It is hopeless, however, and I remain an unconverted infidel. My students typically hold engineering degrees from good schools and many have received Masters Degrees and the occasional Ph.D. from American Universities. They are not stupid people.

Conversations with my students often go somewhat like this:

Jones: You cut off a hand when someone steals. Isn't that cruel and barbaric?

Arab: You imprison thieves and when you let them out, they steal again. America has the highest rate of incarceration in the world. Your black minorities are five times more likely to be imprisoned. Is that what you call civilized? We are not afraid to walk though our cities at night.

Jones: What about beheading in public?

Arab: What about the electric chair? Is that better?

Jones: At least it is not in public.

Arab: So you use it as a deterrent but you don't let anyone see it?

Jones: Your religion allows multiple wives.

Arab: That is our religion; if you can afford them and your first wife lets you (laugh). We do not have unwed mothers. We protect our women. In America, almost 40% of all babies in the USA are born out of wedlock. Almost 75% of black babies are born out of wedlock. Your country has to pay welfare because the mothers cannot support the children and the fathers are not there for them. How is that better?

Jones: You kill drug pushers and people who possess drugs.

Arab: Response: Drug pushers are killing Americans and you cannot stop them. We do not have a drug problem.

Arab: When I lived in America, there were homeless people on the streets of Washington, D.C., begging. You do not see beggars here. The Sheik takes care of them.

Jones: *No response. I have no idea what the Sheik does with them.*

Jones: How can you allow one person, the Sheik, to decide everything for your tribe. Wouldn't you rather have a vote?

Arab: We have a saying here: One man can eat only so much bread. One leader requires only so much money. In America, so many leaders consume too much of your wealth. Also, none of them take full responsibility. Our Sheik holds the power and the responsibility to provide for his people.

Further discussion revealed that there is a hierarchical organization, typically based on age and family relationships, that distributes responsibility and the power throughout the tribe. The tribal structure provides a mechanism for many to participate in decision-making and how wealth is distributed. It is not a simple oligarchy.

The point of relating these exchanges is to show that the differences are great and both sides believe they are right. The Arab is willing to fight to keep the lifestyle he believes in. They think America is lowering the standards of decency and setting a bad example for the rest of the world, which is pretty much, what we think about them. In short, how do you reconcile such huge differences in opinion? These acquaintances are among the most educated people in the Arab world. How do we convince the uneducated to see the world as we do if we cannot convert the brightest? We somehow believe that if we give them the opportunity to have a democracy like ours, they will jump at the chance. It is hard to change the mores and culture of a society, especially if the cultural beliefs are grounded in their religious beliefs and, moreover, they do not want to change. Change, if it comes at all, will be very slow.

The role of women in Arabic society is also foreign to Westerners. While we may not understand why women are not outraged by the lack of personal freedom and equal rights, based upon my experience, the vast majority of Arabic women are not unhappy with the status quo. To be sure, the incidences of stoning or other serious punishment for alleged infidelity as well as lack of educational opportunity are abhorrent. For these and other obvious and serious human rights violations, we Westerners are totally correct in our attempts to protest against these practices and work for change.

However, many women in the Arab world are well cared for and satisfied with their role of mother and wife. They appear to be content to be supported and protected by their husbands or other men in their extended family. We will not change their societal structure in our lifetime, and maybe never.

Significant change will take time. The age of global information, which we are currently experiencing, is the most likely catalyst for change. The internet and other high-speed global communications will expose everyone who has the opportunity to participate to essentially unlimited information. Free exchange of ideas and experiences can eventually overcome dogma and rhetoric for thoughtful, educated people. Time will tell if it will bring Christians and Moslems closer to understanding.

JOHN HAYGOOD

John Haygood earned a B.A. degree in physics at the University of Texas, Austin, and an M.S. degree in Environmental Science, with a major in Health Physics, from the University of Texas Health Science Center at Houston. He is also a Texas Licensed Medical Physicist. He has over 30 years of experience in regulation of radiation use as well as an additional 10 years of consulting in radiation regulatory and safety processes.

Haygood describes how his experiences led up to his concern regarding the weaknesses of radioactive materials security in the United States:

I fell into the world of health physics quite accidently. In 1972, after receiving a bachelor's degree in physics from the University of Texas in Austin, I was seeking employment with the newly created Texas Air Control Board (TACB). I had taken an interest in environmental matters while taking a unique physics course: "Physics of Air Pollution".

After a few months, I received notice from the Texas Department of Health (TDH) that I should come for an interview (the Air Control Board started its existence through TDH and had the same address). I arrived full of excitement in anticipation of getting into interesting work. The person in human resources said that the TACB had its own location, now, and this position was for something else. She invited me to have a seat and said, "I'll notify the Director of Radiation Control that you're here for the interview."

As she walked back to her office, I thought, *Radiation control. How neat! I never realized the government regulated radiation use.* I later found that few people of the time shared that realization.

I began my work with Radiation Control as an x-ray inspector. After a couple of years, since I had a physics degree,

I was moved over to inspection of radioactive material licensed operations. Now life was getting to be very interesting. I was sent to Oak Ridge, Tennessee, for the 10-week health physics course. Oak Ridge was the laboratory that began the research for the atom bomb. It was full of history of the development of radiation research. I also took numerous other courses, such as medical uses, industrial radiography, well-logging use, and so on.

As I learned the inspection process, I was able to travel around the state of Texas and see all types of uses of radiation—under many conditions. Texas was one of two or three of the largest agreement state radiation control programs in the U.S. Texas had at least "one of everything" and a number of uses were developed in the state, as well. This was a great learning opportunity. Life was good!

The working conditions were rather extreme, in many cases. Sometimes I would be working at a major university or medical facility, dressed in coat and tie (during the 70's, it was leisure suits), and the next day I would be out in the desert of south central Texas, digging samples of contaminated soil, in 105° temperatures, for transport to the TDH lab. Or I might be in a meeting with a multi-million dollar company vice-president in the morning, explaining why his company was struggling with safety issues, and then out on an oil drilling rig in south Texas surveying for contaminated materials being returned to the surface due to a source ruptured down-hole—standing there at 2 a.m. in the morning while being pelted with rain, sleet, and snow. Life was great!

I continued working in various areas of radiation control: management, inspections, incident investigation, enforcement, and even licensing—although that was handled by a separate division. Perhaps the most challenging areas were those of uranium mining and waste processing. Around 1979, I had begun participating in "emergency response for fixed nuclear facilities" (nuclear power plant) duties. I spent a great deal of time on the "accident assessment team"—plotting dispersion of radioactive material from release scenarios for the Comanche Peak and South Texas Nuclear Project nuclear power plants. The available computer models were not very good at the time, so I had to write my own programs, but I enjoyed it. For a while they were the only models that worked for us. It was great experience. I retired from TDH in 1997 and consulted in radiation safety for 4 or 5 years. I then returned to TDH and worked in compliance until 2008, when I finally "hung them up". I am thankful for the experience that I received in radiation protection and I enjoyed the task of serving the public by providing such protection.

When Dr. Jones first called me and asked if I would be interested in helping him with a project relating to "dirty bombs", I was ready to dismiss him without much fanfare. However, he sent me materials on work that he had already done in risk assessment in other areas and pointed out the nefarious tactics of terrorists. His arguments were quite compelling. I had been performing "increased controls" inspections for TDH before my final departure in 2008, and felt that the current security controls for large radiation sources were quite stringent and difficult to beat. But after looking at the terrorist techniques and methods that could be applied, I realized that the regulatory efforts had left quite a number of holes in security. I then accepted Dr. Jones offer to work with him on a project of assessing risk and improving security for radioactive materials.

How did I come to the realization that our system of security of radioactive materials was less than "perfect"? It started with the thought of one police officer, armed with only his 9 mm pistol, responding to a call and finding himself face to face with a number of religious fanatics, armed with AK-47's, wearing body armor, carrying hand-grenades, and ready to die for their cause. This scenario made me realize that even the increased controls requirements could easily be futile. Increased controls rely on the response of armed local law enforcement (LEA) to the scene within minutes of notice of penetration of the secured area. That is the final step of security. If it fails, there is no real security for even the largest and most dangerous of sources. I began to realize that an organized plan of stealing a number of lesser sources and using them for dirty bombs would be a viable operation. Or the materials could be used in non-explosion attacks (food and water supplies contamination, for example).

When I first arrived on the regulatory scene in the early 70's, security was aimed more at preventing accident, or preventing theft by persons that did not know the radioactive material that they were trying to steal was a liability—even a danger to them. They would not be able to sell it because those that use it know that a license is required. Often, stolen devices containing radioactive material were found lying beside the road. To dispose of it, one had to pay. It had no value for a thief. Because of circumstances such as these, radiation control inspectors would look specifically for proper securing of radioactive material at all times, whether it was being used, transported, or stored.

As security became more and more of a concern (due to numerous thefts, lost sources, and so forth), I developed my own scheme of evaluating security for licensees that I inspected. It consisted of a "level of security" system (described in Appendix 4) whereby I would count each method the licensee used for securing the radioactive material. If a licensee padlocked the container, placed it into a locked room, and kept the facility locked when unoccupied, I would assign a 3 (a 1 for each method totaled to 3). I would try to encourage each licensee to have a security system that would generate a minimum security level of 3, but preferably 4. Usually, this could be done with little additional expense. To compare this to increased controls of today, our mock evaluations of typical facilities with increased controls resulted in security levels in the 20's and 30's. Other facilities had levels as low as 6.

Facilities using less significant, yet dangerous, radiation sources will still have security levels less than 6.

Industrial radiography, a system that uses large sources (usually Ir-192) to x-ray dense objects, caused many accidents and injuries. We have photographs of serious radiation burns, so horrible looking that the weak of stomach would not want to see them, that resulted from absolutely stupid acts of radiography personnel. Companies hired persons that "maybe" had a high school diploma, trained them quickly, and put them out in the field with the dangerous sources. Fortunately, the requirements for radiographer qualification were greatly increased by more stringent regulations during the 1980's.

Many radiography sources are transported to remote or field sites for use. Well-logging licensees, who use various types of radioactive material to test the subsurface structures that oil, gas, and water wells are drilled into, must transport their sources to remote locations to use them. Moisture density gauge users, must also transport their sources to field locations to test for density and moisture in soils and materials. The portability of these sources allows for easier theft and inadvertent loss. Thus, security has become more and more of an issue for the regulatory agencies.

Before the 1990's, little concern was seen for terrorism uses of radioactive material, although it was "kept in mind". During the 90's, as terrorism began to increase around the world, more concern was given to improving security. However, the concern for security remained more along the lines of preventing casual access and inadvertent loss—although at a higher level. After 9/11 happened, there was a new view of security across the board for all assets and hazardous materials that might be used as weapons. Life had gotten a little shaky.

In 2007, the state and federal radiation regulatory agencies began performing inspections of facilities that were under increased controls. The US NRC provided inspection personnel with a training course on security methods. My electronics training from the US Air Force and my physics background gave me excellent tools for evaluating these processes. None of the licensees that I inspected before leaving the agency in 2008 had a "perfect" program. Even those that were in technical compliance needed a little assistance filling in some "holes". I felt that each was in good shape after either correcting violations or tweaking up their system. After more than 30 years of experience, I was comfortable with the level of security afforded by each program. However, after working on the RAMCAP project with Dr. Jones for the past 2 years, I am now a little concerned about the entire security system. There appears to be too many holes in our security methods. I hope that our new, voluntary Enhanced Security Program (the system is described in Appendix 4) will elevate overall security to a level that will help defeat the terrorists' efforts in the United States. Dr. Jones and I will continue to work towards that end. Life could be great again!

APPENDIX 1

A Primer on the Physics of Radioactive Materials

In this introductory section, which I (Jones) will call Atomic Physics for Dummies, I will attempt to explain what is meant by some of the terms used by physicists. Since I am a mechanical engineer, please excuse technical lapses and homey metaphors.

For the purpose of understanding the basics of elemental physics, let us assume that an **atom** is comprised of only three building blocks.

The first is a **proton**. Think of protons as little round balls, not unlike a ball bearing or a BB. The proton is like a little magnet, which has a positive (+) electric charge. (It is easy to remember that proton is plus (+).)We all have played with magnets and when you put the two positive or two negative ends of magnets together, they repel each other. When you put the opposite poles together, like a positive to a negative, they stick together.

The second building block is called a **neutron**. Neutrons may also be thought of as little balls, like protons, except they do not have an electrical charge. They are neither plus (+) nor minus (-). (Remember **neu**tral, neither +nor—) Think of them as little ball bearings or BB's that are not magnetized.

Now if we group the protons and neutrons together in a small bunch or ball, we have what is called the **nucleus** of the atom. While it is true that the protons are all positively charged and one would think that they would spring apart due to the repelling magnetic forces, the neutrons provide a neutralizing effect. The neutrons are like the glue that holds the protons together.[55]

Thus, the protons and neutrons can live together, in very close quarters, in harmony under certain conditions. It will be seen later that the number of neutrons necessary to hold the nucleus together is approximately equal to the number of protons for elements up to an atomic weight of 20. The neutron and proton have (approximately) the same weight. So now, we have a collection of protons and neutrons, packed very tightly together but not exactly touching, which we will call the nucleus.

The third particle is an **electron**. These speedy little balls of fluff weigh almost nothing and circle the nucleus of an atom. It is not unlike satellites circling the earth, only the electrons are traveling so fast they might look like a blur. It is easier to imagine electrons as little thin shells that surround the nucleus. The electron is moving so fast that all we might see, if we could actually see anything that small, is a blur, like the propeller of an airplane. The electron has a negative charge (-).

The atomic weight of an element is the sum of the protons and the neutrons, since the electrons have almost no mass. The elements are usually placed into a chart, called the periodic Table according to the total mass (weight) of the atom. For example, the carbon atom, which we are very familiar with as coal and another form, more interesting to our wives as a diamond, has a weight of 12. The weight of carbon is the sum of the weight of 6 protons and 6 neutrons. It is usually abbreviated as ^{12}C. The so-called atomic number of carbon is 12. However, carbon can have

---

[55] In the nucleus of the atom, the protons and neutrons bound together by something called the residual strong force. This force is very powerful and overcomes the magnetic repelling force of the proton.

additional neutrons in the nucleus. These neutrons do not affect the way carbon combines chemically with another element[56], but it can affect the nuclear properties of the atom. Thus, we have defined two types of properties that are common to atom behavior, the *chemical* properties, and the *atomic* properties. The chemical properties are what we study in chemistry class. When we combine hydrogen and oxygen in a certain way[57] we can form water, i.e., H_2O. Thus, two hydrogen atoms (H) added to an oxygen atom (O) form a molecule of water. This transformation is the result of a *chemical bond* between the atoms.

Atomic behavior involves the actual structure of the atom, not how it combines chemically with another atom. In fact, the atomic structure of atoms can vary significantly without affecting chemical reactions. We will assume for the remainder of this discussion that the chemical properties of an atom are not influenced by the atomic properties I am about to introduce and thus I will not further discuss chemical behavior.

Atomic behavior, of the type we are interested in, can best be explained by using an example. Most of us have read about archeologists determining the age of their various discoveries using a method called carbon-14 dating. Carbon is one of many elements that have several variations in atomic weight. As discussed earlier, carbon, in its most common form, has six neutrons and six protons. Thus, the atomic weight of carbon is 12 (6N + 6P = 12). However, a small percent of carbon atoms have six protons and seven neutrons and some have six protons

---

[56]   This statement is not exactly true, but it is close enough for this discussion.

[57]   When we burn hydrogen in the air, the heat causes the hydrogen to form a bond with oxygen and water is produced. This demonstrates the concept behind using hydrogen energy to reduce hydrocarbon emission since the byproduct of combustion is water, which is a non-pollutant.

and eight neutrons. These carbon atoms are known as carbon-13 and carbon-14. They are termed **isotopes**[58] of carbon. Physicists prefer the term *nuclide* to describe an atom having a given weight. However, isotope is the older and possibly more common form and I will use it here.

As it turns out, for reasons I do not understand, carbon-12 and carbon-13 are what we call *stable isotopes*. However, carbon-14 is an *unstable isotope* and thus will decay to carbon-12 over time. I like to think of it as the carbon-14 atom has too many neutrons in the nucleus to be totally comfortable. These neutrons are not needed to hold the nucleus together and eventually are thrown out of the nucleus and zip off through space. These unstable atoms are termed **radioactive**. Physicists prefer to call them *radionuclides*.

This degeneration from carbon-14 to carbon-12 may take a long time to happen. Some atoms degenerate more quickly than others. The time to change from one form or isotope to another is measured in terms of its **half-life**. The half-life of an isotope is the time that elapses from the beginning of the measurement to the time for exactly one-half of the material to make the change. For example, the half-life of carbon-14 is 5,730 years (+/—40 years).

Now, knowing this, we can use carbon-14 to date carbonaceous materials. For example, assume an archeologist finds a human bone in a cave and the remains of the fire are present. A sample of the charred wood is subjected to analysis and the amount of carbon-14 that remains in a carefully measured volume is determined. The scientist knows wood normally

---

58   Isotope is a Greek word that means "at the same place". Thus the carbon atom can have different weights but still appear in the "same place" on the chemical periodic table.

contains a very specific number of carbon-14 atoms (actually, the ratio of carbon-14 to carbon-12 atoms) when it is alive, i.e. in plant form. This is because the carbon is obtained by the plants by photosynthesis from carbon dioxide in the atmosphere. (Carbon-14 is produced by cosmic rays impacting nitrogen, thus we have a constant supply of new carbon-14 entering the atmosphere. If it were not for this replenishing of the supply, all of the carbon-14 would have decayed by now.)

Thus, the plant contains approximately the same ratio of carbon-14 as the air when it was alive and growing. By measuring the remaining carbon-14 and knowing how long it takes to transform this isotope to carbon-12, the age of the wood can be determined. It is assumed that the bones are contemporaneous, thus, the site is dated.

The following section (by Haygood), which is admittedly more difficult to understand, provides an additional and more thorough explanation of radioactive materials, the different types of radiation, and how radiation exposure is measured. This information is necessary to the understanding of how radiation damages the human body and how much radiation is too much.

Radioactive material is simply a collection of atoms that are radioactive. These atoms have excess energy and are unstable. Eventually, many give up their excess energy in the form of radiation through a process called decay. In a collection of unstable atoms you cannot predict which will decay next. It is a random process. An unstable atom does not necessarily decay immediately to a stable one. Some will go through a number of decays before they reach a stable form. The original unstable atom is called the *parent*, while the resulting atom is called a *daughter*.

Radioactive atoms are either naturally occurring or manmade. Large complex atoms are formed when stars are made and die. Being generally unstable, over time they decay to less complex ones, which are usually radioactive. Radioactive atoms can be made by exposing certain elements to very high neutron radiation fields, such as found in a nuclear reactor and some accelerators (a machine that electrically produces radiation).

The simplest atom, hydrogen, is constructed of an atom and a proton. The positively charged proton serves as the atom's nucleus while the negatively charged electron orbits at a distance. In this form, the hydrogen atom is balanced and stable. If we add an electron and a proton to the hydrogen atom we create a helium atom. Hydrogen and helium are elements. All matter is composed of elements and each element has the same construction of atoms. If we continue to add electrons, protons, and even neutrons (neutral charge), we obtain heavier and more complex atoms. Adding neutrons changes the stability of the atom. We call these *isotopes*. An isotope is a different form of an element that has the same number of protons in the nucleus but a different number of neutrons.

Radioactive material is often referred to as an *isotope* or *radionuclide*, or as a *radiation source*. In this work, a given isotope will be notated in this form: Cs-137. The Cs indicates the cesium atom, and the "137" indicates the atomic weight of this isotope of cesium. The atomic weight is determined by the sum of the weights of the protons and neutrons in the nucleus. The weights of the electrons are negligible. Cesium has eleven (11) isotopes.

When a radioactive atom decays (transforms), it will do so spontaneously and randomly and it will emit radiation. A collection of atoms of an isotope will have its atoms decaying—but one cannot predict which given atom will decay next. If the radiation coming from the atoms is measured over time, it will be seen that the quantity of emitted radiation will be decreasing.

When half of the atoms have decayed, the radiation level will drop to one-half of the original level. The time required for a given isotope to reduce to the one-half level is called the *half-life*. Each isotope has a unique half-life, which is useful for purposes of identifying unknown isotopes. Cs-137, for example, has a half-life of 30 years.

As indicated above, when a radioactive atom decays (transforms), it will emit some form of radiation. The most common forms of radiation that we deal with are alpha, beta and neutron particles, and gamma radiation (photonic). **Gamma ray photons** are essentially the same as x-rays (commonly produced by x-ray machines). The properties of these radiation forms determine how they are used by mankind. Radiation energy is measured in electron volts. Most commonly, the units will be expressed in multiples of millions of electron volts (Megaelectron volt or MeV), or thousands of electron volts (Kiloelectron volt or KeV).

When a radiation particle or gamma ray interacts with something, such as an air or water molecule, it transfers its energy (some or all) and creates charged particles called ions in a process called **ionization**. We call these radiation forms that can create ions *ionizing radiation*.

Alphas are very large, energetic particles with positive charge that do not travel very far (about 10 cm in air). They can easily be stopped by a piece of paper. They are essentially constructed like the helium atom's nucleus: a particle with two (2) protons and two (2) neutrons. Their energies range from 4-7 MeV. Since the large, energetic particle will interact readily with anything it encounters, it is most hazardous when emitted by a radioactive atom located within a tissue cell.

An **alpha particle** will most likely deposit most of its energy within the cell thereby creating a number of ions. The charged ions will react with cell components thereby changing them. A cell can be damaged by this action sufficiently to cause cell death or the cell may survive the damage. On later cell division, however, the damage may be passed on to the new cells. Alphas cause concern for internal exposure.

Neutrons (large particles with neutral charge) are capable of traveling over 37 km (calculated for fast neutrons) in air. Neutrons, constructed of a proton and an electron bound together, have energies ranging from 0 to greater than 10 MeV. Since neutrons interact well with hydrogen atoms and less well with large atoms, materials with many hydrogen atoms make good shielding material. Neutrons are generally an external exposure concern.

Betas are smaller particles with negative charge that are capable of traveling about 0-10 meters in air. They are physically the same as an electron and their energies can vary from 0-7 MeV. Moderately dense materials, such as plexiglass, are used to provide shielding. When a beta particle interacts with another atom, it can produce an x-ray, which will behave like a gamma ray (see below). Betas can be a concern for both internal and external exposure.

Gamma rays are negligible in size and have neutral charge. They can travel over a 100 meters in air and have energies ranging from 0-5 MeV. X-rays have similar properties, but have an energy range of 0-10 MeV.

Gammas are generated from an atom's nucleus whereas x-rays come from outside of the nucleus. Gamma rays and x-rays are an external exposure concern.

In order to measure radiation, we must have radiation units. International standards for units of measurement for radioactivity and units of measure for radiation exposure have been developed and adopted.

Measurement of radioactivity is based on the number of transformations (also called disintegrations) that occur in a measured time. The unit in current use is the **Becquerel**, or **Bq**, (named after Antoine Becquerel, an early radiation scientist) which is defined as one (1) disintegration per second. This is from the Systeme International[59], or SI, international standard. Previously, the standard unit was the **Curie** (named after Marie Curie, also an early radiation scientist). This unit is from what is commonly called the "traditional" units.

The Curie (Ci) was defined as 3.7×10^{10} disintegrations per second (dps), which is the number of disintegrations per second that 1 gram of Radium-226, in equilibrium with its daughters, exhibits.

In converting and assessing radiation related units, the following unit conversions are frequently used:

Table 1-1—Quantity Conversion Labels

Number	Exponential Expression	Label or prefix
1/1,000,000,000,000	E^{-12}	pico
1/1,000,000,000	E^{-9}	nano
1/1,000,000	E^{-6}	micro
1/1,000	E^{-3}	milli
1	E^{0}	—
1,000	E^{+3}	Kilo
1,000,000	E^{+6}	Mega
1,000,000,000	E^{+9}	Giga
1,000,000,000,000	E^{+12}	Tera

Since the **Becquerel** is an extremely small quantity, we normally use **Terabecquerels** (TBq) to deal with commonly

---

[59]   Wikipedia: The International System of Units (abbreviated SI from French: Système International d'unités) is the modern form of the metric system and is generally a system of units of measurement devised around seven base units and the convenience of the number ten. It is the world's most widely used system of measurement, both in everyday commerce and in science. Wikipedia® is a registered trademark of the Wikimedia Foundation, Inc., a non-profit organization.

encountered quantities. **Gigabecquerels** (GBq) may also be used.

For quantities of radioactivity using the Curie as the unit, we often use pico, nano, micro, milli, Kilo, and Megacuries as units.

Because one may encounter either unit, the conversion is 1 Terabecquerel = 27.03 Curies, and 1 Curie = 0.037 Terabecquerels.

The following tables may help the reader better comprehend the quantities when discussed:

Table 1-2: Conversion of Traditional Radioactivity Units

The Traditional Unit of:	Equals the SI Unit of:
1 picocurie	0.037 Bq
1 nanocurie	37 Bq
1 microcurie	37 KBq
1 millicurie	37 MBq
1 curie	37 GBq
1 Kilocurie	37 TBq
1 Megacurie	37,000 TBq

Table 1-3: Conversion of SI Radioactivity Units

SI Unit of:	Equals the Traditional Unit of:
1 Bq	27.03 picocurie
1 KBq	27.03 nanocurie
1 MBq	27.03 microcurie
1 GBq	27.03 millicurie
1 TBq	27.03 curie

Radioactivity and radiation are two different, but related concerns. Radiation exists as a result of the radioactivity and is our concern when addressing health effects. The radioactivity produces the radiation, which may cause changes in living cells exposed to that radiation. Therefore, we must measure and quantify *exposure* to radiation. Radiation can be measured by detecting and using the number of ion pairs created in the exposed object or target.

A person in a radiation field is exposed to the radiation, but the effect of that exposure must consider the *dose*. The dose takes into account the type of radiation and its particular effect on human tissue. Thus, for measurement of radiation, or radiation levels, we have additional units to consider. The SI units of exposure are **Grays** and **Sieverts**. The Gray (Gy) is the unit of absorbed dose, whereas the Sievert (Sv) is the unit of equivalent dose for all types of radiation. The Sievert allows for a *quality factor* based on the type of radiation. For example, a dose from 100 Gy of gamma radiation does not cause the same effect as a dose of 100 Gy of alpha radiation. The alpha dose causes 10 times the effect, so it has a quality factor of 10 while gamma radiation has a quality factor of 1.

Table 1-4: Regulatory Quality Factors[60]

Type of Radiation	Quality Factor
X, gamma, or beta radiation and high-speed electrons	1
Alpha particles, multiple-charged particles, fission fragments and heavy particles of unknown charge	20
Neutrons of unknown energy	10
High-energy protons	10

The traditional units for exposure and dose are **Roentgen** (R), Radiation Absorbed Dose (**RAD**), and rem (or **REM**). The roentgen[61] is a unit of measurement for exposure to ionizing radiation (such as X-ray and gamma rays), and is named after the German physicist Wilhelm Roentgen. The RAD[62] (Radiation Absorbed Dose) is the amount of radiation causing a material to absorb 100 ergs per gram of material.

The REM[63] is the roentgen (or radiation) equivalent in man (or mammal) and is a unit of radiation dose equivalent. The Quality Factor, as in Table 1-4, is used to convert the RAD to REM or rem. The relationship between the rem and the Sievert is:

60   Haygood, John R.: "RADIATION SAFETY HANDBOOK—Regulatory Processes Explained," 2nd Edition, 2001, P. 2-10.
61   Wikipedia: 1 R is the amount of radiation required to liberate positive and negative charges of one electrostatic unit of charge (esu) in 1 cm³ of dry air at standard temperature and pressure (STP). This corresponds to the generation of approximately 2.08×10^9 ion pairs.
62   Haygood, John R.: P. 2-12.
63   Wikipedia: REM is the product of the absorbed dose in rads and a weighting factor (or Quality Factor, Q), WR, which accounts for the effectiveness of the radiation to cause biological damage.

1 Sv = 100 rem = 100,000 mrem

or

1 rem = 0.01 Sv = 10 mSv

In summary, radioactive material is composed of unstable atoms and presents radioactivity. The presence of the radioactivity produces radiation, which can expose other matter. The exposure of the other matter deposits energy in that matter and produces ions—charged particles that can cause changes in the matter exposed.

APPENDIX 2 ━━━━━━━━━━━━━━━━━━━━━━━

Glossary of Frequently Used Terms

Alpha particle (symbol α) A large, high-energy particle consisting of two protons and two neutrons bound together into a particle identical to a helium nucleus.[A]

Atom a basic unit of matter that consists of a dense, central nucleus surrounded by a cloud of negatively charged electrons.[A]

Beta particle (symbol β) A high-energy, high-speed electron or positron emitted by certain types of radioactive nuclei.[A]

Chain reaction, nuclear A condition where one nuclear reaction causes an average of one or more nuclear reactions, thus leading to a self-propagating number of these reactions. The specific nuclear reaction may be the fission of heavy isotopes, such as U-235.[A]

Critical mass The smallest amount of fissile material needed for a sustained nuclear chain reaction. [A]

Criticality The point at which neutrons being released by fissioning of fissionable atoms, thereby causing fissioning of additional atoms, reach a constant rate during a nuclear chain reaction.

Decay, radioactive The spontaneous breakdown of an atomic nucleus, an unstable nucleus that does not have enough binding energy to hold itself together, resulting in the release of energy and matter from the nucleus.[B]

Decay, biological The metabolic elimination processes (excretions) which reduce the amount of radionuclide in the body without regard to the radioactive decay.

Disruptive radiation device A disruptive radiation device is a weapon composed of an explosive material and radioactive material and combined in a manner that an explosion can result in mass disruption.

Electron A subatomic particle carrying a negative electric charge with no known components or substructure; generally thought to be an elementary particle.[A]

Electron volt (eV) The amount of kinetic energy gained by a single unbound electron when it accelerates through an electric potential difference of one volt. 1 keV is 1000 electron volts and 1 MeV is 1 million electron volts. Used to express the energy of particles, particularly radiation particles.[A]

Element A pure substance consisting of one type of atom distinguished by its atomic number (number of protons in its nucleus).[A]

Fissile material A material that is capable of sustaining a chain reaction of nuclear fission.[A]

Fission A process where an atom with a large atomic nucleus (such as uranium) is split into two or more smaller particles.

Fissionable material A nuclide that is capable of undergoing fission after capturing either high-energy (fast) neutrons or low-energy thermal (slow) neutrons.[C]

Gamma (ray) (symbol γ) High-energy, short wavelength, electromagnetic radiation (a packet of energy) emitted from the nucleus. Gamma radiation frequently accompanies alpha and beta emissions and always accompanies fission. Gamma rays are very penetrating and are best stopped or shielded by dense materials, such as lead or uranium. Gamma rays are basically the same as X-rays, differing in their source and their energy ranges.[D]

Half-life, radiological The time in which one half of the atoms of a particular radioactive substance disintegrates into another nuclear form. Measured half-lives vary from millionths of a second to billions of years. Also called physical half-life.[D]

Half-life, biological The time required for the body to eliminate one half of the material taken in by natural biological means.

Half-life, effective The time required for the amount of a radioactive element deposited in a living organism to be diminished 50% as a result of the combined action of radioactive decay and biological elimination.

Health physicist A person who works in the area of environmental health engineering/physics that deals with the protection of the individual and population groups against the harmful effects of ionizing and non-ionizing radiation.

Improvised Explosive Device (IED) A "homemade" bomb constructed and deployed in ways other than in conventional military action. It may be constructed of conventional military explosives, such as an artillery round, attached to a detonating mechanism. Also known as a roadside bomb.[A]

Infrastructure The basic physical and organizational structures needed for the operation of a society or enterprise, or the services and facilities necessary for an economy to function. The term typically refers to the technical structures that support a society, such as roads, water supply, sewers, electrical grids, telecommunications, and so forth.[A]

Isotope One of two or more atoms with the same number of protons, but different numbers of neutrons in their nuclei. Thus, carbon-12, carbon-13, and carbon-14 are isotopes of the element carbon, the number denoting the approximate atomic weights. Isotopes have very nearly the same chemical properties, but often different physical properties (for example, carbon-12 and—13 are stable, while carbon-14 is radioactive).[D]

Naturally Occurring Radioactive Materials (NORM) Materials consisting of radioactive elements found in the environment, such as uranium, thorium and potassium and any of their decay products, such as radium and radon.

Neutron An uncharged elementary particle with a mass slightly greater than that of the proton and found in the nucleus of every atom heavier than hydrogen.[D]

Neutron activation Is the process whereby neutron radiation induces radioactivity in materials. The resulting atoms can be of the same isotope, or a different one, and are usually radioactive.

Nuclear power plant An electric power generating facility that uses fissioning of atoms to generate heat.

Nuclear weapon A device (atom bomb) that uses fissioning of atoms to generate a massive explosion. A thermo-nuclear weapon uses an atom bomb to cause fusion of hydrogen atoms, thereby creating a more massive explosion.

Photon An elementary particle and the basic unit of light and of all other forms of electromagnetic radiation.[A]

Proton A subatomic particle, stable by itself, with a positive electric charge.[A]

Radiation, Ionizing Any radiation capable of displacing electrons from atoms or molecules, thereby producing ions. Alpha, beta, gamma, X-rays, and neutrons are forms of ionizing radiation.[D]

Radioactive material Any material (solid, liquid, or gas) that emits radiation spontaneously.[D]

Radioactive Material Dispersal Device (RDD) An RDD is a speculative radiological weapon that combines radioactive material with conventional explosives. It is also known as a "dirty bomb". The purpose of the weapon is to contaminate the area around the explosion with radioactive material, hence the attribute "dirty".

Radioactivity The spontaneous emission of radiation, generally alpha or beta particles, often accompanied by gamma rays, from the nucleus of an unstable isotope.

Weapon of Mass Disruption (MDW) A weapon designed to radioactively contaminate an area, thereby disrupting man's activities in the area. It is unlikely to cause large numbers of fatalities or serious injuries, but it could have devastating economic consequences.

Weapon of Mass Destruction (WMD) A nuclear warhead or atomic bomb that uses either fission or fusion of highly refined nuclear materials to create a massive explosion.

X-ray Penetrating electromagnetic radiation (photon) having a wavelength that is much shorter than that of visible light. These rays are usually produced by excitation of the electron field around certain nuclei. Photons originating in the nucleus of an atom are gamma rays, and those originating in the electron field of an atom are X-rays. [D]

Definitions were taken from the following resources:

[A] Wikipedia. Wikipedia® is a registered trademark of the Wikimedia Foundation, Inc., a non-profit organization. Acquired online, 05/2011.

[B] NDT Education Resource Center, Brian Larson, Editor, 2001-2011, The Collaboration for NDT Education, Iowa State University, www.ndt-ed.org. Acquired online, 05/2011.

[C] US NRC glossary, online, acquired 06/2011.

[D] Haygood, John R.: "RADIATION SAFETY HANDBOOK—Regulatory Processes Explained," 2nd Edition, 2001, Glossary.
.
[E] Jones, J. William; Nickell, Robert E.; Haygood, John R.: "Methodology for Assessing Risk from Radioactive Materials Found in Medical, Industrial and Academic Sites"; ASME Innovative Technologies Institute, LLC, March 2011.

APPENDIX 3

SOME ISOTOPES* THAT
TERRORISTS MIGHT USE

1. **Isotope: Americium-241 (241Am) and Am(Be)-241**

Am-241 has a half-life of 430 yrs. Its principal emissions are alpha (α) and beta (β) particles and gamma (γ) rays. The alpha particle is the most energetic (α 5.5 MeV), the beta is moderately energetic (β 0.52 MeV), and the gamma is weak (γ 0.033 MeV). The specific activity is 3.5 Ci/g. Am-241 is ranked as Hazard Class I (Very High Hazard Potential) on the Relative Hazard Potential Classification Group table.

Americium is a malleable, silvery white metal that tarnishes slowly in dry air at room temperature. It is typically quite insoluble; although a small fraction can become soluble through chemical and biological processes. It does not occur naturally but is produced artificially by successive neutron capture reactions of plutonium isotopes. There are sixteen known isotopes of

---

*   Note - Excerpts from: "Radiological and Chemical Fact Sheets to Support Health Risk Analyses for Contaminated Areas", Argonne National Laboratory Environmental Science Division, John Peterson, Margaret MacDonell, Lynne Haroun, and Fred Monette, U.S. Department of Energy Richland operations Office, R. Douglas Hildebrand and Chicago Operations Office, Anibal Taboas, March 2007.

americium and all of them are radioactive, but only three have half-lives long enough to warrant concern: americium-241, americium-242m, and americium-243. Of these, americium-241 is generally the most prevalent isotope in use. It decays by emitting an alpha particle with attendant gamma radiation.

For internal exposure, americium can be taken into the body by eating food, drinking water, or breathing air. Gastrointestinal absorption from food or water is a likely source of internally deposited americium in the general population. After ingestion or inhalation, most americium is excreted from the body within a few days and never enters the bloodstream; only about 0.05% of the amount taken into the body by ingestion is absorbed into the blood. After leaving the intestine or lung, about 10% clears the body. The balance enters the bloodstream and deposits about equally in the liver and skeleton where it remains for long periods of time, with biological retention half-lives of about 20 and 50 years, respectively. The weak gamma emission of americium-241 decay offers a very low external exposure hazard. The major health concern is tumors resulting from the ionizing radiation emitted by americium isotopes deposited on bone surfaces and in the liver.

Am-241 is used extensively in industry. There is some use in academics, but currently little use in the medical community. A very common use of americium is in smoke detectors where the alpha particle associated with the decay of americium-241 is used to ionize the air. Alpha particles from smoke detectors do not themselves pose a health hazard, as they are absorbed in a few centimeters of air or by the structure of the detector. Americium is also used as a common neutron source by combining the americium-241 and beryllium atoms. The alpha particle given off during the radioactive decay of americium-241 is absorbed by beryllium-9 atoms, producing carbon-12 and a neutron. Large americium-241 neutron sources are used extensively in well-logging (gas and oil industry) and smaller ones are used for gauging devices. Most use is probably in portable/mobile devices, but small quantities (about 40 mCi) are used. **Am-241 is offered online.**

Terrorists might acquire Am-241 by theft from storage facilities, while in transport, or while in use in the field (usually remote areas). Am-241 is one of the most transported radioactive isotopes. Once acquired, free Am-241 could be converted to a soluble form and introduced to water supplies or food to cause internal exposure. Large Am-241 neutron sources can be placed in areas where humans may spend a great deal of time to cause large external exposures. Americium-241 could not readily be used to create immediate radiation exposure symptoms, such as "burns" or even death. Its use would be to threaten cancers later in life.

2.   Isotope: Californium-252 (Cf-252)

Cf-252 has a half-life of 2.6 years. Its principal emissions are alphas, betas, and gammas. The alphas are very energetic (α 5.9 MeV), while the betas and gammas are very weak, (β 0.0056 MeV) and (γ 0.0012 MeV), respectively. Cf-252 has a specific activity of 540 Ci/g. It is ranked as Hazard Class I (Very High Hazard Potential) on the Relative Hazard Potential Classification Group table.

Californium is a silvery-white or gray metal with a density somewhat greater than that of lead. It is typically quite insoluble. Californium, which does not occur naturally, is produced artificially in nuclear reactors and particle accelerators. Ten isotopes of californium are known to exist and all are radioactive, however, only five have half-lives long enough to be of concern: Cf-248, Cf-249, Cf-250, Cf-251, and Cf-252. The half-lives of these isotopes range from 0.91 to 900 years, while those of the other isotopes are less than two months. All five of these isotopes decay by emitting an alpha particle, and all but Cf-248 also decay by spontaneous fission (SF). About 3% of the radioactive decays of Cf-252 are by SF, while only a very small fraction of the decays of the other three isotopes are by SF. Cf-252 is a very strong neutron emitter, with one microgram emitting 170 million neutrons per minute.

For internal exposure, californium can be taken into the body by eating food, drinking water, or breathing air. Gastrointestinal absorption from food or water is a likely source of internally deposited californium in the general population. After ingestion or inhalation, most californium is excreted from the body within a few days and never enters the bloodstream; only about 0.05% of the amount taken into the body by ingestion is absorbed into the blood. After leaving the intestine or lung, about 65% of the californium that does enter the bloodstream deposits in the skeleton, 25% deposits in the liver, and the rest deposits in other organs or is excreted, primarily in urine. The biological half-lives in the skeleton and liver are about 50 and 20 years, respectively. Californium in the skeleton is deposited on bone surfaces and slowly redistributes throughout the bone volume over time. Cf-252, with about 3% of the decays by spontaneous fission, is a significant source of neutrons and gamma rays and can cause significant external exposures.

Currently, the only californium isotope that has a commercial use is Cf-252. Because this radionuclide is only available in very small quantities its uses are quite limited. Cf-252 is a very strong neutron emitter, with one microgram emitting 170 million neutrons per minute. Thin foils containing californium-252 can be used as a source of fission fragments for research purposes. Californium-252 can also be used as a portable neutron source to identify gold or silver ores through neutron activation analysis, and it can be used in moisture gauges to locate water and oil-bearing layers in oil wells. Cf-252 has been used in trailered devices for highway/bridge evaluation. In addition, californium-252 has been used in brachytherapy to treat various types of cancer. **Cf-252 is offered online.**

Terrorists might acquire Cf-252 by theft from storage facilities or while in transport. Once acquired, it could be converted to a soluble form and introduced to water supplies or food to cause internal exposure. Large Californium-252 sources can be placed in areas where humans may spend a great deal of time to cause large external neutron exposures. Californium-252 could not readily be used to create immediate radiation exposure symptoms, such as "burns"—or even death. Its use would be to threaten cancers later in life.

3. Isotope: Cobalt-60 (Co-60)

Co-60 has a half-life of 5.3 years. It has principal emissions of betas and gammas. The gammas are very energetic (γ 2.5 MeV) while the betas are of moderate energy (β 0.097 MeV). It has a specific activity of 1100 Ci/g. It is ranked as Hazard Class II (High Hazard Potential) on the Relative Hazard Potential Classification Group table.

Cobalt is a hard, silvery-white metal that occurs in nature as cobalt-59. It is usually found in association with nickel, silver, lead, copper, and iron. Pure cobalt metal is prepared by reducing its compounds with aluminum, carbon, or hydrogen. It is similar to iron and nickel in its physical properties. Cobalt has relatively low strength and little ductility at normal temperatures and is a component of several alloys. It is typically insoluble. It can be made soluble through chemical and biological processes.

There are nine major radioactive cobalt isotopes. Of these, only Co-57 and Co-60 have half-lives long enough to warrant concern. The two energetic gamma rays that accompany the radioactive decay of Co-60 make this isotope an external hazard. Co-60 is produced by neutron activation of components in nuclear reactors; it can also be produced in a particle accelerator. When an atom of uranium-235 (or other fissile nuclide) fissions, it generally splits asymmetrically into two large fragments—fission products with mass numbers in the range of about 90 and 140—and two or three neutrons. A number of reactor components are made of various alloys of steel that contain chromium, manganese, nickel, iron and cobalt, and these elements can absorb neutrons to produce radioactive isotopes, including cobalt-60. Co-60 is a radionuclide of concern in spent nuclear fuel (as a component of the fuel hardware) and in the radioactive wastes associated with nuclear reactors and fuel reprocessing plants.

Co-60 poses both an internal and external hazard, and the main health concern is associated with the increased likelihood of cancer. Inside the body, cobalt presents a hazard from both beta and gamma radiation. Cobalt can be taken into the body by eating food, drinking water, or breathing air. Gastrointestinal absorption from food or water is the principal source of internally deposited cobalt in the general population. Estimates of the gastrointestinal absorption of cobalt range from 5 to 30%, depending on the chemical form and amount ingested; 10% is a typical value for adults and 30% for children. Of the cobalt that deposits in the liver and other tissues, 60% leaves the body with a biological half-life of 6 days and 20% clears with a biological half-life of 60 days; the last 20% is retained much longer, with a biological half-life of 800 days. On the basis of animal studies, retention of cobalt was determined to be the same for all age groups. Inhaled cobalt oxide moves from the lung to body tissues quite readily. Calculation of internal dose can be rather complicated. Inhalation poses a higher risk than ingestion. External exposure is a concern because of the strong external gamma radiation, and shielding is often needed to handle wastes and other materials with high concentrations of the isotope. Calculation / measurement of doses due to external exposures is rather easy and straightforward. The major health concern is cancer, later in life, resulting from the exposure to the ionizing radiation.

High-energy gamma rays emitted during the radioactive decay of Co-60 can be used to detect flaws in metal components and in brachytherapy to treat various types of cancer. (Brachytherapy is a method of radiation treatment in which sealed sources are used to deliver a radiation dose at a distance of up to a few centimeters by surface, intracavitary, or interstitial application.) Co-60 is also the principle isotope used in sterilization irradiators—wherein mega-curies of Co-60 sealed sources are situated to yield extremely high radiation fields. **Co-60 is offered online.**

Terrorists could acquire Co-60 by theft from use and/or storage facilities, while in transport, or while in use in the field (usually remote areas). Once acquired, Co-60 could be chemically converted to a soluble form and introduced to water supplies or food to cause internal exposure. The more likely use would be to set large Co-60 sources in areas where humans may spend a great deal of time to cause large external exposures. Co-60 can be used to create immediate radiation exposure symptoms, such as "burns"—even death. Its use would also threaten cancers later in life.

4.   Isotope: Cesium-137 (Cs-137)

Cs-137 has a Half-life of 30 years. Its principal emissions are a beta (β 0.19 MeV) from the daughter Ba-137m (2.6 min half-life) for 95% of the decays and another beta (β 0.065 MeV), and a gamma (γ 0.60 MeV). Cs-137 has a specific activity of 3.5 Ci/g (540 million for Ba-137m). It is ranked as Hazard Class III (Moderate Hazard Potential) in the Relative Hazard Potential Classification Group table.

Cesium is a soft, silvery white-gray metal that occurs in nature as cesium-133. The natural source yielding the greatest quantity of cesium is the rare mineral pollucite. Although it is a metal, cesium melts at the relatively low temperature of 28o C (82o F), so like mercury it is liquid at moderate temperatures. This most alkaline of metals reacts explosively when it comes in contact with cold water.

Radioactive Properties: There are 11 major radioactive isotopes of cesium. Only three have A-6 half-lives long enough to warrant concern: Cs-134, Cs-135 and Cs-137. Each of these decays by emitting a beta particle, and their half-lives range from about 2 to 2 million years. The half-lives of the other cesium isotopes are less than two weeks. Of these three, the isotope of most concern is Cs-137 which has a half-life of 30 years. Its decay product, barium-137m, with a half-life of about 2.6 minutes, stabilizes itself by emitting an energetic gamma ray. Cesium radionuclides are fission products, with Cs-135 and Cs-137 being produced with relatively high yields of about 7% and 6%, respectively. That is, about 7 atoms of Cs-135 and 6 atoms of Cs-137 are produced per 100 fissions. Cs-137 is a major radionuclide in spent nuclear fuel, highlevel radioactive wastes resulting from the processing of spent nuclear fuel, and radioactive wastes associated with the operation of nuclear reactors and fuel reprocessing plants.

Cesium can be taken into the body by eating food, drinking water, or breathing air, and behaves in a manner similar to potassium whereby it distributes uniformly throughout the body. Essentially all cesium that is ingested is absorbed into the bloodstream through the intestines. Cesium tends to concentrate in muscles because of their relatively large mass. Like potassium, cesium is excreted from the body fairly quickly. In an adult, 10% is excreted with a biological half-life of 2 days, and the rest leaves the body with a biological half-life of 110 days. Clearance from the body is somewhat quicker for children and adolescents.

If someone is exposed to radioactive cesium and the source of exposure is removed, much of the cesium will readily clear the body along the normal pathways for potassium excretion within several months. Cs-137 presents an external as well as internal health hazard. The strong external gamma radiation associated with its short-lived decay product barium-137m makes external exposure a concern, and shielding is often needed to handle materials containing large concentrations of Cs-137. While in the body, cesium poses a health hazard from both beta and gamma radiation, and the main health concern is associated with the increased likelihood for inducing cancer.

In applications, Cs-137 is often used as cesium-chloride (a water soluble material) in steel encapsulations. Cs-137 is used in brachytherapy to treat various types of cancer. (Brachytherapy is a method of radiation treatment in which sealed sources are used to deliver a radiation dose at a distance of up to a few centimeters by surface, intracavitary, or interstitial application.) In industrial applications, Cs-137 is used in the same manner as Co-60. Often, one or the other will be selected for a given application based on its specific properties. **Cs-137 is offered online.**

Terrorists might acquire Cs-137 by Theft from storage facilities, while in transport, or while in use in the field (usually remote areas). Cs-137 can be used to target both internal and external exposures. External exposure from large sources is probably more likely. Cs-137 in soluble form can be introduced to water supplies or food to cause internal exposure. Large Cs-137 sources can be placed in areas where humans may spend a great deal of time to cause high external exposures. Cs-137 can be readily used to create immediate radiation exposure symptoms, such as "burns"—or even death. Its use could also be to threaten cancers later in life.

5. Isotope: Iridium-192 (Ir-192)

Ir-192 has a half-life of 74 days. Its principal emissions are a beta and a gamma. The beta (β 0.22 MeV) is quite energetic and the gamma (γ 0.82 MeV) is very energetic. Ir-192 has a specific activity of 9200 Ci/g. It is in the Hazard Class III (Moderate Hazard Potential) of the Relative Hazard Potential Classification Group table.

Iridium is a silvery white metal. It is hard and brittle with low ductility, which makes it very difficult to machine and form. It is quite dense—about twice as dense as lead. As a very corrosion resistant metal, iridium is quite insoluble in water.

There are 15 major radioactive iridium isotopes, but only three have half-lives longer than a month: Ir-192, Ir-192m, and Ir-194m. The half-lives of the other isotopes are less than 2 weeks. Ir-192 has a half-life of 74 days, decaying to stable platinum-192 and osmium-192 by emitting a beta particle and by electron capture. Ir-192 is the most commonly used of the iridium isotopes and it has a high specific activity and significant gamma radiation. Ir-192 is the isotope of most concern based on general availability as it is used in a number of industrial and medical applications.

Iridium can be taken into the body by eating food, drinking water, or breathing air. Gastrointestinal absorption from food or water is the likely source of internally deposited iridium in the general population. After ingestion or inhalation, most iridium is excreted from the body and never enters the bloodstream; only about 1% of the amount taken into the body by ingestion is absorbed into the blood. Twenty percent of the iridium that reaches the blood is excreted right away, 20% deposits in the liver, 4% deposits in the kidney, 2% deposits in the spleen, and the remaining 54% is evenly distributed among other organs and tissues of the body. Of the iridium that deposits in any organ or tissue, 20% leaves the body with a biological half-life of 8 days and 80% clears with a biological half-life of 200 days. On the basis of animal studies, retention of iridium was determined to be the same for all age groups. Most inhaled iridium compounds appear to clear the lungs quite rapidly. Iridium can concentrate in several organs depending on its chemical form, so while there is no dominant organ of health concern the liver is a main organ of deposition. Inside the body, these iridium isotopes can pose a hazard from both beta and gamma radiation. External exposure is a concern because of the strong gamma radiation (especially for Ir-192 and Ir-194m), and shielding is needed to handle Ir-192 radiographic and medical sources. The iridium isotopes pose both an internal and external hazard, and the main health concern is associated with the increased likelihood of cancer. **Ir-192 is offered online.**

Ir-192 is used extensively in industry. It is a major tool of industrial radiography, where 100+ curie sources are transported around the county for X-raying dense objects. There is some use in medicine and academics.

Terrorists could acquire Ir-192 by theft from storage facilities, while in transport, or while in use in the field (usually remote areas). Once acquired, large Ir-192 sources can be placed in areas where humans may spend a great deal of time to cause large external exposures, such as populated areas like shopping malls and transportation devices like subways, buses, etc. It would have to be converted into "dust" size particles, or solubilized, to introduce to water supplies or food to cause internal exposure. Iridium-192 could be a "choice tool" for terrorism. Ir-192 can be used to create immediate radiation exposure symptoms, such as "burns"—or even death. Exposure would also threaten cancers later in life.

6. Isotope: Promethium-147 (Pm-147)

Pm-147 has a half-life of 2.62 years. Its principal emission is a beta (β 0.225 MeV, max). It has a specific activity of 930 Ci/g. It's ranked as Hazard Class III (Moderate Hazard Potential) in the Relative Hazard Potential Classification Group table.

Promethium is a silver-white metal not found in the Earth's surface. It has a melting point of 1,160°C (2,120°F) and no measured boiling point. Its density is 7.2 grams per cubic centimeter. Little is yet generally known about the properties of metallic promethium. Ion exchange methods led to the preparation of about 10 g of promethium from atomic reactor fuel processing wastes in early 1963.

Seventeen isotopes of promethium, with atomic masses from 134 to 155 are now known and Pm-147 is the most generally useful. Pm-145 is the longest lived, and has a specific activity of 940 Ci/g. Pm-147 is a soft beta emitter. Although no gamma rays are emitted, X-radiation can be generated when beta particles impinge on elements of a high atomic number, and great care must be taken in handling it. Promethium salts luminesce in the dark with a pale blue or greenish glow, due to their high radioactivity.

Promethium can be taken into the body by eating food, drinking water, or breathing air. Since Pm-147 is a soft beta emitter, exposure would only be internal. The soft beta emission of the Pm-147 offers a very low external exposure hazard. The major health concern is tumors resulting from the internal exposure of tissues.

Promethium has limited uses. It can be used as a source of power. The radiation it gives off provides energy, similar to that from a battery. A promethium battery can be used in places where other kinds of batteries would be too heavy or large to use, as on satellites or space probes. Such batteries are far too expensive for common use, however. Promethium is also used to measure the thickness of materials. For example, suppose thin sheets of metal are being produced on a conveyor belt. A sample of promethium metal is placed above the metal and a detector is placed below. The detector counts the amount of radiation passing through the metal. If the metal sheet becomes too thick, less radiation passes through. If the sheet becomes too thin, more radiation passes through. The detector reports when the sheet of metal is too thick or too thin. It can automatically stop the conveyor belt when this happens. Some compounds of promethium are luminescent. Luminescence is the property of giving off light without giving off heat. The light of a firefly is an example of luminescence. Promethium compounds are luminescent because of the radiation they give off. **Pm-147 is offered online** (Switzerland).

The terrorist might acquire Pm-147 through theft from storage facilities or while in transport. Once acquired, free Pm-147 could be converted to a soluble form and introduced to water supplies or food to cause internal exposure. Promethium-147 could not readily be used to create immediate radiation exposure symptoms, such as "burns"—or even death. Its use would be to threaten cancers later in life.

7. Isotope: Plutonium-238 (Pu-238), Plutonium-239 (Pu-239), Plutonium(Beryllium)-239 [Pu(Be)-239]

Pu-238 has a half-life of 88 years and Pu-239 has one of 24,000 years. The principal emissions of Pu-238 are high energy alpha (α 5.5 MeV) and low energy beta (β 0.011 MeV) particles and low energy gamma rays (γ 0.0018 MeV). Pu-239 has principal emissions of high energy alpha (α 5.1 MeV) and low energy beta (β 0.0067 MeV) particles and low energy gammas (γ < 0.001 MeV). Their specific activities are Pu-238-17 Ci/g and Pu-239-0.063 Ci/g. Pu-238 and Pu-239 are ranked as Hazard

Class I (Very High Hazard Potential) on the Relative Hazard Potential Classification Group table.

Plutonium in its pure form is a very heavy, silver-colored, radioactive metal about twice as dense as lead.

Essentially all of the plutonium on earth has been created within the past six decades by human activities involving fissionable materials. The most common form in the environment is plutonium oxide. Plutonium is typically very insoluble, with the oxide being less soluble in water than ordinary sand (quartz). It adheres tightly to soil particles and tends to remain in the top few centimeters of soil as the oxide. In aquatic systems, plutonium tends to settle out and adhere strongly to sediments, again remaining in upper layers. Typically one part of plutonium will remain in solution for every 2,000 parts in sediment or soil. A small fraction of plutonium in soil can become soluble through chemical or biological processes, depending on its chemical form. While plutonium can bioconcentrate in aquatic organisms, data have not indicated that it biomagnifies in aquatic or terrestrial food chains.

Several plutonium isotopes exist, all of which are radioactive. Except for Pu-241, these isotopes decay by emitting an alpha particle. Pu-241 decays to americium-241 by emitting a low-energy beta particle. Am-241 is much more radiotoxic than its parent. The maximum activity of Am-241 is about 3% of the initial activity of Pu-241 and occurs 73 years later. An extremely small fraction of the decays of Pu-236, Pu-238, Pu-240, and Pu-242, are by spontaneous fission (SF), as are about 0.1% of the Pu-244 decays. Pu-242 and Pu-244 are generally present in relatively minute activity concentrations.

When plutonium is inhaled, a significant fraction can move from the lungs through the blood to other organs, depending on the solubility of the compound. Little plutonium (about 0.05%) is absorbed from the gastrointestinal tract after ingestion, and little is absorbed through the skin following dermal contact. After leaving the intestine or lung, about 10% clears the body. The rest of what enters the bloodstream deposits about equally in the liver and skeleton where it remains for long periods of time, with biological retention half-lives of about 20 and 50 years, respectively, per simplified models that do not reflect intermediate redistribution. The amount deposited in the liver and skeleton depends on the age of the individual, with fractional uptake in the liver increasing with age. Plutonium in the skeleton deposits on the cortical and trabecular surfaces of bones and slowly redistributes throughout the volume of mineral bone with time. The weak beta and gamma emissions of the Pu-238 and Pu-239 offer a very low external exposure hazard. Plutonium generally poses a health hazard only if it is taken into the body because all of its isotopes, except Pu-241, decay by emitting an alpha particle, while the beta particle emitted by Pu-241 is of low energy. Minimal gamma radiation is associated with these radioactive decays. However, there is an external gamma radiation hazard associated with Pu-244 from its short-lived decay product neptunium-240m. Inhaling airborne plutonium is the primary concern for all isotopes, and cancer resulting from the ionizing radiation is the health effect of concern. The ingestion hazard associated with common forms of plutonium is much lower than the inhalation hazard because absorption into the body after ingestion is quite low. Laboratory studies with experimental animals have shown that exposure to high levels of plutonium can cause decreased life spans, diseases of the respiratory tract, and cancer. The target tissues in those animals were the lungs and associated lymph nodes, liver, and bones. However, these observations in experimental animals have not been corroborated by epidemiological investigations in humans exposed to lower levels.

The nuclear properties of Pu-239, as well as the industry's ability to produce large amounts of nearly pure Pu-239, led to its use in nuclear weapons and nuclear power. The fissioning of uranium-235 in the reactor of a nuclear power plant produces two to three neutrons, and these neutrons can be absorbed by U-238 to produce Pu-239 and other isotopes. Pu-239 can also absorb neutrons and fission along with the U-235. Plutonium fissions provide about one-third of the total energy produced in a typical commercial nuclear power plant. The use of plutonium in power plants occurs without it ever being removed from the nuclear reactor fuel, i.e., it is fissioned in the same fuel rods in which it is produced. Another isotope, Pu-238, is used as a heat source in radiothermal generators to produce electricity for a variety of purposes including unmanned spacecraft and interplanetary probes. The United States recovered or acquired about 110,000 kilograms (kg) of plutonium between 1944 and 1994, and about 100,000 kg remains in inventory. Of this amount, over 80%is in the form of weapons grade plutonium, primarily Pu-239. Plutonium was generated in production reactors at DOE's Hanford and Savannah River sites, and weapons components were produced at the Rocky Flats facility. Surplus plutonium is currently stored at the Pantex Plant and other sites. Pu-239 has been combined with beryllium to create neutron sources, in the same manner as the Am(Be)-241neutron sources. **Pu-239 is offered online.**

Terrorists might acquire plutonium by theft from storage facilities, while in transport, or while in use in the field (usually remote areas). The chance of removal from nuclear power plants or weapons facility is probably very remote. A more likely method would be theft from Pu(Be)-239 sources—found at educational facilities and some industrial operations. Fortunately, most of these have been removed from public use and secured by DOE. Otherwise, plutonium would probably have to be imported from other countries with less rigorous controls. Once acquired, plutonium could be converted to a soluble form and introduced to water supplies or food to cause internal exposure. Large Pu-239/Be neutron sources can be placed in areas where humans may spend a great deal of time to cause large external exposures. Pu(Be)-239 sources could not readily be used to create immediate radiation exposure symptoms, such as "burns"—or even death. Its use would be to threaten cancers later in life.

8. Isotope: Radium-226 (Ra-226)

Ra-226 has a half-life of 1600 yrs and its specific activity is 1.0 Ci/g. The principal emissions of Ra-226 are energetic alpha (α 4.8 MeV) and low energy beta (β 0.0036 MeV) particles and low energy gammas (γ 0.0067 MeV). Ra-226 is ranked Hazard Class I (Very High Hazard Potential) on the Relative Hazard Potential Classification Group table.

Radium is a radioactive element that occurs naturally in very low concentrations (about one part per trillion) in the earth's crust. In its pure form, it is a silvery-white heavy metal that oxidizes immediately upon exposure to air.

Radium was first discovered in 1898 by Marie and Pierre Curie, and it served as the basis for identifying the activity of various radionuclides. One curie of activity equals the rate of radioactive decay of one gram (g) of Ra-226. Ra-226 is a radioactive decay product in the uranium-238 decay series and is the pre cursor of radon-222. Ra-228 is a radioactive decay product in the thorium-232 decay series. Both isotopes give rise to many additional short-lived radionuclides, resulting in a wide spectrum of alpha, beta and gamma radiations. Lead-210, which has a 22-year half-life, is included in the list of short-lived radionuclides associated with Ra-226 for completeness, as this isotope and its short-lived decay products are typically present with Ra-226. Ra-226 decays by emitting an alpha particle. Ra-228 has a much shorter half-life (5.8 years) and decays by emitting a beta particle. While Ra-226 poses a hazard due to its long half-life, Ra-228 poses a long-term hazard only if its parent (thorium-232) is present. Radium has a density about one half that of lead and exists in nature mainly as Ra-226, although several additional isotopes are present. It is present in all uranium and thorium minerals; its concentration in uranium ores is about one part radium to 3 million parts uranium. The chemical properties of radium are similar to those of barium, and the two substances are removed from uranium ore by precipitation and other chemical processes. Originally, radium was obtained from the rich pitchblende ore found in Bohemia. The carnotite sands of Colorado furnish some radium, but richer ores are found in the Republic of Zaire and the Great Lake Region of Canada. Radium is a major contaminant in mine and milling wastes, such as uranium mill tailings, and is present in various radioactive wastes associated with past uranium processing activities.

Radium can be taken into the body by eating food, drinking water, or breathing air. Most of the radium taken in by ingestion (about 80%) will promptly leave the body in feces. The remaining 20% enters the bloodstream and is carried to all parts of the body. Inhaled radium can remain in the lungs for several months and will gradually enter the bloodstream and be carried throughout the body. The metabolic behavior of radium in the body is similar to that of calcium. For this reason, an appreciable fraction is preferentially deposited in bone and teeth. The amount in bone decreases with time from the exposure, generally dropping below 10% in a few months to 1% and less in a few years. Release from the bone is slow, so a portion of inhaled and ingested radium will remain in the bones throughout a person's lifetime. The inhalation risk is associated primarily with radium decay products, i.e., radon and its short-lived daughters. Each of the two radium isotopes decays into a gaseous radon isotope. Radon-222 is a short-lived decay product of Ra-226, and radon-220 is a short-lived decay product of Ra-228. The primary hazard associated with radon arises from the inhalation of its short-lived decay products, which are charged ions that readily attach to dust particles. These particles can be inhaled into the lungs and deposited on the mucous lining of the respiratory tract. Unattached decay products tend to be inhaled deeper into the lungs where the residence time is longer. When alpha particles are then emitted within the lung, the cells lining the airways can be damaged, potentially leading to lung cancer over time. The strong external gamma radiation associated with several short-lived decay products of Ra-226 and Ra-228 makes external exposure a concern, and shielding is often needed to handle waste and other materials containing large concentrations of these radionuclides. The majority of epidemiological data on the health effects of Ra-226 and Ra-228 in humans comes from studies of radium dial painters, radium chemists, and technicians exposed through medical procedures in the early 1900s. These studies, as well as studies on experimental animals, indicate that chronic exposure to radium can induce bone sarcomas. The minimum latency period is seven years after the first exposure, but tumors can continue to appear throughout a lifetime.

Ra-226 is the only radium isotope used commercially. Historically, the main use of radium has been as a component in luminous paint used on the dials of watches, clocks, and other instruments, although it is no longer used for this purpose. While Radium was often used in brachytherapy to treat various types of cancer, there is probably little such use, today. (Brachytherapy is a method of radiation treatment in which sealed sources are used to deliver a radiation dose at a distance of up to a few centimeters by surface, intracavitary, or interstitial application.) Radium was also used in gauging devices and oil field activities, but these uses, too, have been greatly reduced. Most Radium today is probably stored and waiting for disposal resources to develop. **Ra-226 is offered online.**

Terrorists might acquire Ra-226 by theft from use or storage facilities or while in transport. Once acquired, Ra-226 could be converted to a soluble form and introduced to water supplies or food to cause internal exposure. Large Ra-226 gamma sources can be placed in areas where humans may spend a great deal of time to cause large external exposures. Although Radium is in a state of slowly being removed from society, it would make a good weapon for both internal and external exposure. Ra-226 can also be easily extracted from the environment by a person knowledgeable in chemistry.

9.   Isotope: Selenium-75 (Se-75)

Se-75 has a half-life of 119.8 days and a Specific Activity of 20-45 Ci/g. Its principal emission is gammas (γ 0.280 MeV, average, 0.800 MeV max). Se-75 has not been assigned to a class in the Relative Hazard Potential Classification Group table.

Selenium is a non-metallic mineral that resembles sulfur and can exist as a gray crystal, red powder, or vitreous black form. It exists as an elemental or metal compound. It is a volatile, reactive, and corrosive element chemically resembling sulfur and forming extremely toxic compounds. It has moderate density (4.3 g/cm3 to 4.8 g/cm3) and melts at 217°C.

Selenium occurs in nature as six stable isotopes. Se-80 is the most prevalent, comprising about half of natural selenium. The other five stable isotopes and their relative abundances are: Se-74 (0.9%); Se-76 (9.4%); Se-77 (7.6%); Se-78 (24%); and Se-82 (8.7%). There are nine major radioactive selenium isotopes. The half-life of Se-75 is 120 days and the half-lives of all other isotopes are less than eight hours. Se-75 decays by electron capture with a half-life of 119.8 days to stable arsenic-75, emitting an average of 1.75 gamma rays with an average energy of 215 keV each, and a peak energy of 800 keV.

Selenium can be taken into the body by eating food, drinking water, or breathing air. Gastrointestinal absorption is the principal source of internally deposited selenium in the general population. About 80% of selenium incorporated in food and soluble inorganic compounds are absorbed from the gastrointestinal tract into the bloodstream. However, elemental selenium and selenides are relatively inactive biologically, and only about 5% of these forms are absorbed from the intestines. After reaching the blood, selenium selectively deposits in the liver (15%), kidneys (5%), spleen (1%) and pancreas (0.5%). The remainder is deposited uniformly throughout all other organs and tissues. Of the selenium deposited in any organ or tissue, 10% is retained with a biological half-life of 3 days, 40% is retained with a biological half-life of 30 days, and 50% is retained with a biological half-life of 150 days. As a gamma emitter, internal exposure caused by ingested selenium would be minimal. External exposure to Se-75 is a concern because of the strong external gamma radiation, and shielding is needed to handle high concentrations of the isotope. Calculation and measurement of doses due to external exposures is rather easy and straightforward. The major health concern is cancer, later in life, resulting from the exposure to the ionizing radiation. Sources used in radiography are large enough to cause serious injury, even death.

Se-75 is used in radiography cameras to x-ray thin-walled structures and, until recently, was not commonly used in the United States. With recent Ir-192 shortages, Se-75 has seen increased use. **Se-75 is offered online.**

Terrorists can acquire Se-75 by theft from storage facilities, while in transport, or while in use in the field (usually remote areas). Once acquired, terrorists might find the best use of Se-75 as a terror weapon is to use it as a source of external radiation—such as hiding large sources in public places or on transportation systems, thereby causing serious external exposures.

10. Isotope: Strontium-90 (Sr-90) [Yttrium-90 (Y-90)]

Note: The main health concerns for Sr-90 are related to the energetic beta particle from Y-90, thus they will be discussed together.

Sr-90 has a Half-life of 29 years and Y-90 has a half-life of 64 hours. The specific activities are Sr-90—140 Ci/g, and Y-90—550,000 Ci/g. The principal emissions of Sr-90 are betas (β 0.20 MeV) and those of Y-90 are high energy betas (β 0.94 MeV) and weak gammas (γ negligible). Sr-90 is ranked Hazard Class I (Very High Hazard Potential) on the Relative Hazard Potential Classification Group table.

Strontium is a soft, silver-gray metal that occurs in nature as four stable isotopes. It is a reactive metal typically found as an oxide or a salt.

Sixteen major radioactive isotopes of strontium exist, but only Sr-90 has a half-life sufficiently long (29 years) to warrant concern. The half-lives of all other strontium radionuclides are less than 65 days. Sr-90 decays to Y-90 by emitting a beta particle, and Y-90 decays by emitting a more energetic beta particle with a half-life of 64 hours to zirconium-90. The main health concerns for Sr-90 are related to the energetic beta particle from Y-90. While four stable isotopes of strontium occur naturally, Sr-90 is produced by nuclear fission. When an atom of uranium-235 (or other fissile nuclide) fissions, it generally splits asymmetrically into two large fragments—fission products with mass numbers in the range of about 90 and 140—and two or three neutrons. (The mass number is the sum of the number of protons and neutrons in the nucleus of the atom.) Sr-90 is such a fission product, and it is produced with a yield of about 6%. That is, about six atoms of Sr-90 are produced per 100 fissions. Sr-90 is a major radionuclide in spent nuclear fuel, high-level radioactive wastes resulting from processing spent nuclear fuel, and radioactive wastes associated with the operation of reactors and fuel reprocessing plants.

Strontium can be taken into the body by eating food, drinking water, or breathing air. Gastrointestinal absorption from food or water is the principal source of internally deposited strontium in the general population. On average, 30 to 40% of ingested strontium is absorbed into the bloodstream. The amount absorbed tends to decrease with age, and is higher (about 60%) in children in their first year of life. Adults on fasting and low-calcium diets can also increase intestinal absorption to these levels, as the body views strontium as a replacement for calcium. Strontium behaves similarly to calcium (although it is not homeostatically controlled, i.e., the body does not actively regulate levels within the cells), but living organisms generally use and retain it less effectively. For adults, about 31% of the activity entering the blood (plasma) from the gastrointestinal tract is retained by bone surfaces; the remainder goes to soft tissues or is excreted in urine and feces. Much of the activity initially deposited on bone surfaces is returned to plasma within a few days based on an updated biokinetic model that accounts for redistribution in the body. About 8% of the ingested activity remains in the body after 30 days, and this decreases to about 4% after 1 year. This activity is mainly in the skeleton. Sr-90 concentrates in bone surfaces and bone marrow, and its relatively long radioactive half-life (29 years) make it one of the more hazardous products of radioactive fallout. The health effects associated with Sr-90 were studied concurrent with development of the atomic bomb during World War II by the Manhattan Engineer District. Bone tumors and tumors of the blood-cell forming organs are the main health concern. These tumors are associated with the beta particles emitted during the radioactive decay of Sr-90 and Y-90. External gamma exposure is not a major concern because Sr-90 emits no gamma radiation and its decay product Y-90 emits only a small amount. Strontium is a health hazard only if it is taken into the body. Sr-90 concentrates in bone surfaces and bone marrow, and its relatively long radioactive half-life (29 years) make it one of the more hazardous products of radioactive fallout. The health effects associated with Sr-90 were studied concurrent with development of the atomic bomb during World War II by the Manhattan Engineer District. Bone tumors and tumors of the blood-cell forming organs are the main health concern. These tumors are associated with the beta particles emitted during the radioactive decay of Sr-90 and Y-90.

Sr-90 has been used as an isotopic energy source in various governmental research applications, including in radiothermal generators to produce electricity for a variety of purposes including devices to power remote weather stations, navigational buoys, and satellites. Sr-90 has been used in medical plaques for certain eye treatments. No evidence found that Sr-90 is offered online.

Terrorists can acquire Sr-90 by theft from storage facilities, while in transport, or while in use. Once acquired, the "best" use for terrorism might be to put Sr-90 in a form to be introduced to food and water supplies.

11. Isotope: Thulium-170 (Tm-170)

Tm-170 has a half-life of 130 days. It has a specific activity of 40-400 kBq/g. Its principal emissions are betas (β 0.315 MeV, average 0.967 MeV, max) and gammas (γ 0.084 MeV). It is assigned to Hazard Class II (High Hazard Potential) in the Relative Hazard Potential Classification Group table.

Thulium is a silvery metal so soft it can be cut with a knife. It is easy to work with and is both malleable and ductile. Its melting point is 1,550°C (2,820°F) and its boiling point is 1,727°C (3,141°F). Its density is 9.318 grams per cubic centimeter. Thulium is relatively stable in air. That is, it does not react easily with oxygen or other substances in the air. It does react slowly with water and more rapidly with acids.

Only one naturally occurring isotope of thulium exists, thulium-169. It is not radioactive. At least 16 radioactive isotopes of thulium are also known.

There is not very much literature available for Tm-170. Most dose will occur in the lungs. High external exposures can be experienced. Burns and immediate death caused by high external exposures are possible. Long term prospect of cancer is a possible outcome of exposure.

Tm-170 is useful as a radiation source for a thickness gauge for metal, or as a density gauge. It can be used in gamma radiography. **Tm-170 is offered online**.

Terrorists can acquire Tm-170 by theft from storage facilities, while in transport, or while in use in the field (usually remote areas). Once acquired, it can be used to cause high external exposures in the same manner as other sources used in radiography.

12. Isotope: Ytterbium-169 (Yb-169)

Yb-169 has a half-life of 32 days. Its specific activity is 2.2×10^4 Ci/g. Its principal emission is gammas (γ 0.093 MeV—mean). Yb-169 not listed on the Relative Hazard Potential Classification Group table.

Ytterbium is a soft, malleable, ductile, lustrous silver-white metal. Although it is one of the rare-earth metals of the lanthanide series in Group 3 of the periodic table, in some of its chemical and physical properties it more closely resembles calcium, strontium, and barium. It exhibits allotropy; at room temperature a face-centered cubic crystalline form is stable. The metal tarnishes slowly in air and reacts slowly with water but rapidly dissolves in mineral acids. It forms numerous compounds, some of which are yellow or green. The oxide (ytterbia) is colorless. It is widely distributed in a number of minerals, e.g., gadolinite, and is recovered from monazite but has no commercial uses. Metallic ytterbium dust poses a fire and explosion hazard.

Naturally occurring ytterbium is composed of 7 stable isotopes, Yb-168, Yb-170, Yb-171, Yb-172, Yb-173, Yb-174, and Yb-176, with Yb-174 being the most abundant (31.83% natural abundance). Twenty-seven radioisotopes have been characterized, with the most stable being Yb-169 with a half-life of 32.026 days, Yb-175 with a half-life of 4.185 days, and Yb-166 with a half life of 56.7 hours. All of the remaining radioactive isotopes have half-lives that are less than 2 hours, and the majority of these have half-lives that are less than 20 minutes. This element also has 12 meta states, with the most stable being Yb-169m (t ½ 46 seconds). The isotopes of ytterbium range in atomic weight from 147.9674 u (Yb-148) to 180.9562 u (Yb-181). The primary decay mode before the most abundant stable isotope, Yb-174 is electron capture, and the primary mode after is beta emission. The primary decay products before Yb-174 are element 69 (thulium) isotopes, and the primary products after are element 71 (lutetium) isotopes. Of interest to modern quantum optics, the different ytterbium isotopes follow either Bose-Einstein statistics or Fermi-Dirac statistics, leading to interesting behavior in optical lattices.

The gamma emission of Yb-169 would make it more of an external exposure hazard. As an external exposure hazard, Yb-169 exposures are rather simple to measure and calculate. The major health concern is cancer, later in life, resulting from the exposure to the ionizing radiation. However, external exposures can be high enough to cause burns and perhaps death.

Yb-169 is being examined for use in brachytherapy and there is some use in radiography. **Yb-169 is offered online.**

Terrorists might acquire Yb-169 by theft from storage facilities, while in transport, or while in use in the field (usually remote areas). Once acquired, large Yb-169 sources can be placed in areas where humans may spend a great deal of time to cause large external exposures.

13. Polonium-210 (Po-210):

Note: The following information is adapted from [65]the IAEA Factsheet on Po-210.

Polonium-210 (Po-210) is a radioactive element that occurs naturally and is present in the environment at extremely low concentrations. It is a fairly volatile (50% is vaporized in air in 45 hours at 55°C) silvery-grey soft metal. Po-210 has a half-life of 138 days. This is the time it takes for the activity to decrease by half due to a process of radioactive decay. Po-210 decays to stable lead-206 by emitting alpha particles, accompanied by very low intensity gamma rays. The majority of the time Po-210 decays by emission of alpha particles only, not by emission of an alpha particle and a gamma ray.

Being produced during the decay of naturally occurring uranium-238, polonium-210 is widely distributed in small amounts in the earth's crust. Although it can be produced by the chemical processing of uranium ores or minerals, uranium ores contain less than 0.1 mg Po-210 per ton. Because Po-210

---

[65]   http://www.iaea.org/Publications/Factsheets/English/polonium210.html

is produced from the decay of radon-222 gas, it can be found in the atmosphere from which it is deposited on the earth´s surface. Although direct root uptake by plants is generally small, Po-210 can be deposited on broad-leaved vegetables. Deposition from the atmosphere on tobacco leaves results in elevated concentrations of Po-210 in tobacco smoke. There are tiny amounts of Po-210 in our bodies.

Po-210 can be manufactured artificially by irradiating stable bismuth-209 with thermal neutrons resulting in the formation of radioactive Bi-210, which decays (half-life 5 days) into Po-210. Polonium may now be made in milligram amounts in this procedure which uses high neutron fluxes found in nuclear reactors. Only about 100 grams are produced each year, making polonium exceedingly rare.

Po-210 is used in neutron sources (where it is mixed or alloyed with beryllium). It is also used in devices that eliminate static electricity in machinery where it can be caused by processes such as paper rolling, manufacturing sheet plastics, and spinning synthetic fibers. Brushes containing Po-210 are used to remove accumulated dust from photographic films and camera lenses. Static eliminators typically contain from one to tens of GBq of radioactivity.

Po-210 emits so many alpha particles each second that the energy released from one gram is 140 watts, and a capsule containing about half a gram will spontaneously reach a temperature of 500°C. As a result it has been used as a lightweight heat source to power thermoelectric cells in satellites. A Po-210 heat source was also used in each of the Lunokhod rovers deployed on the surface of the Moon, to keep their internal components warm during the lunar nights. However, because of its short half-life Po-210 cannot provide power for long-term space missions and has been phased out of use in this application. Polonium is not subject to IAEA safeguards.

Po-210 is highly radioactive and chemically toxic element. Direct damage occurs from energy absorption into tissues from alpha particles. As an alpha-emitter Po-210 represents a radiation hazard only if taken into the body. It is important to note that alpha particles do not travel very far—no more than a few centimeters in air. They are stopped by a sheet of paper or by the dead layer of outer skin on our bodies. Therefore, external exposure from Po-210 is not a concern and Po-210 does not represent a risk to human health as long as Po-210 remains outside the body. Most traces of it on a person can be eliminated through careful hand-washing and showering.

Po-210 can enter the body through eating and drinking of contaminated food, breathing contaminated air or through a wound. The biological half-time (the time for the level of Po-210 in the body to fall by half) is approximately 50 days. If taken into the body, Po-210 is subsequently excreted, mostly through feces but some is excreted through urine and other pathways. People who come into contact with a person contaminated by Po-210 will not be at risk unless they ingest or inhale bodily fluids of the contaminated person.

Of the approximately 520 incidents reported by States to the IAEA's Illicit Trafficking Data Base since 2004, 14 incidents have involved industrial Po-210 sources. Three of these incidents occurred in 2006. The incidents involved the theft, loss, or disposal of static eliminators and air ionizers containing sealed Po-210 sources. Po-210 used in these sealed sources is bound with other materials and extraction of the Po-210 would require some chemical treatment in a laboratory. **Po-210 is offered online.**

APPENDIX 4

Voluntary Security Program Highlights

Appendix 4 contains the following information which has been developed for use by licensees who participate in a voluntary program to enhance security. This enhanced security program as presented below is preliminary and will require additional effort to complete, pilot at a number of facilities, and make available to licensees.

* Enhanced Security Program—a description of a program of security assessment.
* Assessment of Security Status—steps to be taken to assess a security program and enter the information on the screening document.
* Screening Document—a checklist screening document that allows one to assess a program and develop a level of security value.
* Security Level Screening Test Examples
* Screening Results of 11 Example Programs

ENHANCED SECURITY PROGRAM
for MIAN FACILITIES

This proactive program is a screening process that enables possessors of radioactive material to voluntarily assess their own level of security and make modifications to enhance security to higher levels, if necessary or desirable.

The steps of the enhanced security program (ESP) consist of:

1. Using a screening tool to assess the current security level.
2. Using an assessment tool to determine the risk that any of the radioactive material might be used as a weapon.
3. Using an assessment tool to determine the consequences and cost should the radioactive material be successfully deployed as a weapon.
4. Compare to acceptance requirement based on category. (Yes: stop; No: go to step 5)
5. Employing additional security measures in the facility's security plan to reduce the potential risk for the material being used as a weapon.
6. Repeating 1-4 until the risks and consequences are reduced to an acceptable level.

ESP includes the use of Increased Controls (IC) for Category 1 and 2 radioactive materials required by government regulations. It also includes Category 3 and Category 4 radioactive materials, but does not include Category 5.

Increased Controls require radioactive material licensees, as a minimum, to:

1. Control access to radioactive material quantities of concern
2. Monitor and detect unauthorized access
3. Control licensed material during transport
4. Physically control portable/mobile devices
5. Maintain documentation of controls

6. Protect sensitive information from unauthorized disclosure

ESP addresses "levels of security", where one level of security is a device and/or method designed to prevent access. For example, a source stored in a locked container would be one level of security.

Some examples of individual methods providing one level of security are:

*   Locked device or container
*   Device/container chained or positively secured to structure or is physically part of structure
*   Locked door to area
*   Locked building
*   Locked fence around site
*   Video/audio surveillance
*   Guard
*   Alarmed/monitored security system
*   Presence of authorized personnel

Thus, placing a locked container in a locked room, in a locked building, inside of a locked fenced area, with a security guard on duty 24 hours per day, would provide a total of 5 levels of security. Personnel in attendance would be one level, as would an operable intruder alert system. On the other hand, a system of background checks would not be counted, but should be considered under the overall security plan of the facility. Not all locked features would be counted as one security level. If a room was used to store radioactive material and the room had two locked doors, only one security level exists. Either door could be penetrated so there is only one level of security. It is also anticipated that the locks being used are effective. Control of keys and codes must be considered.

It is anticipated that radioactive material could be removed from the possession of a licensee by one of the following:

- Diversion of shipment to/from site
- Inside employee removes
- Theft
- Armed attack team

Ideally, a certain level of security could be set to prevent any of the above methods from being successful. Unfortunately, almost all facilities are different and a given level which is successful for one facility may be inadequate for the next. Thus, each facility should be evaluated on its own merits with the security levels being used as guides.

There are many methods of deploying any stolen radioactive material, but the most likely methods would be drawn from:

- Explosive dispersal of sealed sources
- Placement of individual or clustered sources in transportation system or public areas, such as schools, universities, and government offices
- Radioactive material removed from cladding and placed in dispersible condition—dispersed by explosion
- Radioactive material removed from cladding and placed in dispersible (water soluble) condition—dispersed into water or food supply (schools, universities, commercial businesses, public venues, and government offices could be targeted)
- Perpetrators hide material in unknown location and use fear to terrorize the public

The consequences and costs of the deployment of radioactive material through one of these mechanisms should be evaluated so that the efforts of preventing removal and deployment will be expended in the areas with greatest consequence.

For storage, use, and/or transport circumstances, the selected security methods from the following lists should be employed in a manner that renders unauthorized removal to be highly unlikely.

Active Methods:

- Security plan/program
- Security training for personnel
- System of authorizing access (background checks)
- Monitoring/alarm system.
- Video/audio surveillance
- Guard
- Method to deploy armed local law enforcement (LLEA)
- Presence of authorized personnel
- Periodic inspection/inventory

Passive Methods:

- Locked device
- Locked container
- Container chained or positively secured to structure
- Locked metal (steel) cage
- Locked door to room of use or storage
- Locked building
- Locked fence around site
- Device/container physically part of structure
- Device position in structure (such as elevated on platform)

Each licensee (a possessor of radioactive material must have a license issued by the US NRC or an Agreement State) should employ a number of these security methods to minimize the possibility of unauthorized removal. A licensee under increased controls, for example, would probably employ the following, as a minimum:

- Security plan/program
- Security training for personnel
- System of authorizing access
- Monitoring/alarm system
- Method to deploy armed local law enforcement (LLEA)
- Periodic inspection/inventory
- Locked device/container
- Container chained or positively secured to structure
- Locked door to room of use or storage
- Locked building
- Locked fence around site

Assuming that the value of each security level is one (1), this would yield a security level of about eleven (11). A licensee NOT under increased controls but possessing a gauging device with a very large source would probably employ the following, as a minimum:

- Security plan/program or a system of authorizing access
- Periodic inspection/inventory
- Locked device/container
- Container chained or positively secured to structure
- Locked door to room of use or storage
- Locked fence around site

This would only be a security level of about 6 or 7. In most cases, experience indicates a security level of 3 or 4 is typical for non-IC licensees. This program presents a weighted scheme of security levels. Some security measures are more valuable/effective than others in prevention, or at least slowing down, unauthorized access. In most circumstances, an armed security guard would be far more effective than a padlock—even a heavy duty one. Thus, weighting of the security devices/methods will be employed to better estimate the overall security level. The weighting of the various methods will be presented in the screening tool.

A screening tool has been developed to assess the security level for each source, to assess the risk that it might be used as a weapon, and to assess the consequences and cost should the source be successfully deployed as a weapon. The licensee should apply the screening tool to each source possessed that exceeds one (1) IAEA D-level. If the screening process indicates that the security level is too low and/or that the risk of it being used as a weapon and/or that the cost/consequences would be unacceptably high, then additional security steps may need to be employed. Site security has a large impact on the overall risk to the public regarding the use of radioactive material for terrorist purposes. One of the key parameters that will reduce overall risk is to reduce the probability of obtaining the material for malicious purposes. While it is impossible to completely eliminate the possibility of theft, armed attack, and other extreme means of obtaining material at all sites, good security practices can greatly reduce this probability.

Notes:
- Health effects and acute injuries can be included separately as non-monetary items or included in monetary costs by assigning a reasonable numerical value for life and/or acute injury.

- Remediation cost should include clean-up cost and replacement / repair of structures and damaged items to bring the facility back to original condition.
- Cost of denial of service should be included as a first-order effect.
- Cascading effects to second order level should be included in cost of consequences. Examples of cascading effects include:

1. Food/water contamination, where 1st order = deaths and acute injuries and 2nd order = losses to the serving establishment and suppliers of products affected by the event;

2. Explosion used to disseminate radioactive material, where 1st order = deaths and acute injuries, plus damage to structures and remediation costs and 2nd order = losses due to denial of service, loss of income, and effects on suppliers and customers; and

3. Placement on public transportation, where 1st order = deaths and acute injuries, damage to equipment, and denial of service, and 2nd order = loss of income for passengers and employers, including time lost at jobs and costs of alternate transportation for the duration of service denial. Note that 3rd level cascading could include loss of future business, effects on product brand names, losses at second-tier suppliers (e.g., restaurants in the general area, dry cleaners, public services in general, customer satisfaction, etc.). These costs are not included since they are more difficult to estimate and depend on the resiliency of the affected area to recover from the event.